WHAT FRUIT are you BEARING?

Women Walking in the Fruit of the Spirit

AN ANTHOLOGY FROM ANOINTED WOMEN OF GOD
presented by
CAROLYN W. SCOTT AND MONE'T S. HORTON

Thank you for your services and contributions:

Cover design and photography by:
Annette E. Morton
Life Thoughts Graphics
Life Thoughts Photography
© All rights reserved.
www.lifethoughtspublishing.com
*Headshots: Vonzella Faulk, Jacqueline Ejim, E. Love Cookley,
Andrea Taylor and Katherine T. Parker

Photography by:
Aisha Butler
Jazzy Studios Photography
*Headshots: Mone't Horton, Moniette Laury,
Carolyn Scott and Carla Scott

Editing Support by:
Tiera Parker, MSW

Collaboration Management by:
Mone't S. Horton
Mo's Enterprise
www.mos-enterprise.com

Unless otherwise noted, all Scripture quotations are taken from the
King James Version of the Holy Bible.

"But the fruit of the Spirit is love, joy, peace, longsuffering, kindness, goodness, faithfulness, [23] gentleness, self-control. Against such there is no law."

Galatians 5:22-23 NKJV

TABLE OF CONTENTS

DEDICATION

I cannot begin to tell it all, but I want to dedicate this collaboration to the many leaders, mentors, pastors and apostles who played an intricate role in my spiritual growth, walk with the Lord and life as a whole. I thank God for each and every one of them for their prayers, guidance, instruction, correction and push have brought me to this birthing moment.

Pauline Young, Mentor

Leah White, Pastor

(Greater Faith Baptist Church)

Apostles, Michael & Kathy Berkley, Pastors

(Agape Faith Christian Center Ministries International)

Winnie Gilliam, Founding Pastor

(St. Paul Apostolic Holiness Church)

Dr. Mackie J. Cookley, Pastor & Rev. Lucille Cookley

(Coakleys Community Baptist Church)

Katherine T. Parker, Apostle

(On Time Church Ministries Inc.)

Chief Apostle Samuel A. Wright III, Pastor

(Grace Restoration Life Christian Fellowship Inc.)

Pastor Carolyn W. Scott
Visionary

ACKNOWLEDGMENTS

I Thank God for each co-author who has taken the time to participate in this visionary work! Both my biological and spiritual daughters for catching hold of the vision, you thought it not robbery to commit your time, energies, gifts, and talents to partake with me in the vision. I deeply appreciate your Yes and pray that the Lord continues to bless your ministries and endeavors as you submit to Him.

A special Thank You to my granddaughter, miracle baby, Mone't S. Horton for your administrative oversight, coordination, and coaching throughout this process. Now I know why God had me to pray like Hannah—against all odds— as your mother carried you in her womb.

It has been a long time coming, but it is due season and God has ordained this release.

To God be the Glory!

Pastor Carolyn W. Scott
Visionary

FOREWORD

Apostles Michael and Dr. Kathy Berkley are called out and chosen by God to lead Pastors and we teach them to grow up a people who would hear God's voice and obey. Our discipleship and training were with Dr. Eleanor Bryant Graham. We have been in ministry since 1989, Pastoring, training, doing workshops, conferences, and counseling.

Pastor Carolyn Scott has been an Ordained Minister with Agape Faith Christian Center since 2003. She has trained and ministered at annual conferences; her subject matter dealt with building up the inner man and she loved intercessory prayer. There is no doubt that much prayer has gone into every page of this book and lives will be changed if you allow the fruits of the spirit to bloom in your life. Pastor Carolyn has encouraged women and families to grow in Christ and learn how to love one another to reap great rewards in the kingdom. She has been an advocate for ministering and perfecting those desiring to know more about themselves and improving their lives to accomplish greater endeavors in their lifetime.

Pastor Carolyn has been with Agape Faith Christian Center Ministries International and has served her ministry in the Baltimore City area, where she Pastored her street ministry. Every year she grew more faithful because she wanted her calling and purpose to the Kingdom of God to be productive and assist those that God has chosen her to serve. Those that she ministered to were discipled and taught to be fruitful in the spirit because Pastor Carolyn knew that to be saved and not growing in Christ was not enough; there was more. This book has been written for the more that she desires for those who have a hunger for getting closer and developing themselves into servants that God can use and trust.

Pastor Carolyn Scott is a prayer warrior that we have known for over 35 years. She has always had a love for people and desires to help anyone who is downtrodden and in need. Pastor Carolyn has walked in the fruit of the Spirit. She is a pillar of love and peace; we know her to be "Sold Out" for the Lord (Loving Christ Eternally).

We Love You Carolyn,
Apostles Michael & Kathy Berkley
Agape Faith Christian Center Ministries International

INTRODUCTION

"And he shall be like a tree planted by the rivers of water, that bringeth forth his fruit in his season; his leaf also shall not wither; and whatsoever he doeth shall prosper."

Psalm 1:3

The Power of the Seed

Everything starts with a seed. When planted, the seed needs the proper and prepared soil to mature to the point of producing fruit. If you plant the seed, it must be watered to keep the soil moist to produce fruit.

Let us look at a picture of a pack of seeds. We trust that when the seeds are planted, they will produce the picture that is shown on the outside. For example, an apple, we know how many seeds are in an apple, but we really cannot calculate how many apples are in the seed.

Do you know what is inside of you?

If seeds stay in the pack, there is no growth or harvest. The pack must be opened, the seeds poured out and planted into the prepared, good, and fertile soil to experience growth and harvest.

Fruit symbolizes abundance, fertility, plenty, and harvest. Fruit are evidence of the power producing it.

> *11 And God said, Let the earth bring forth grass, the herb yielding seed, and the fruit tree yielding fruit after his kind, whose seed is in itself, upon the earth: and it was so. 12 And the earth brought forth grass, and herb yielding seed after his kind, and the tree yielding fruit, whose seed was in itself, after his kind: and God saw that it was good.*
>
> Genesis 1:11-12 KJV

v

***Why did God choose fruit and not vegetables to describe
"fruit of the Spirit?"***

Fruit are not a vegetable. Fruit are seed bearing structures
that develop from the ovary of a flowering plant. A vegetable on
the other hand consists of all the other plant parts such as roots,
leaves and stems.

Fruit can heal major diseases, relieve pain, give energy, and
regulate blood pressure. Fruit help to maintain, fight, repair,
treat, stimulate, boost, promote, reduce, and improve all
nutrients needed for a healthy body.

Fruit can be used for different purposes, occasions, and
seasons. Some fruit are bitter, sweet, but they have their own
personal taste that satisfies the cravings of the appetite. Fruit
have their own unique qualities—varying in color, shape, texture,
and sizes. They maintain their original design, distinct function,
intent, and purpose— while still having commonalities that allow
them to complement one another when served together in a fruit
salad, pleasant to taste.

Liken to fruit, God has an original design, distinct function,
intent, and purpose for your life. Guess what? You will not fully
live the life He has intended until you answer His call.

Do you know what fruit you are bearing?

Let us walk together on this journey of empowerment and
transformation, walking in the *fruit of the Spirit.*

Apostle Katherine T. Parker

PRAYER

God, we thank you for this occasion that you have been waiting for. You knew in your time it would be birthed forth. As we embark on this journey, we thank you for reminding us of how we ought to represent you. We thank you for your long suffering towards us that you give us time and love us back to where we need to be in you. We thank you that this is a milestone, and we mark it down as a memorial. They say, *"What would Jesus do?"* This moment, this movement of the Holy Spirit—not a show, but a flow. This will remind us to be slow to speak, swift to hear. That we may not anger Oh God. This will remind us that we will not do what the Father did not give us instructions to do. We thank you God for helping us now to trust you more. That our emotions will be stabilized. Our spirit will be FREE and transformed.

We thank you that our mind will be renewed. We thank you for the surgery that will take place on the inside that we will not go out the way we came in! We commit this movement into your hands. You can keep that which we commit unto you against this day. We pray that you give every co-author a fresh oil anointing even that which they have studied and written will flow off the page and bring life, illumination, transformation, and application to every reader. Holy Spirit drown them deep and go past that! In the name of Jesus.

We thank you that we will see the *fruit of the Spirit* in a way that we have never seen it hither to before. We thank you for the voices, we thank you for the vessels and God you be honored with this movement. In the mighty name of Jesus. We bless you. We thank you for the visionary. Please continue to strengthen and encourage her heart. Let this be a spiritual 4th of July that will

blast her off into other dimensions and realms of ministry that you have given unto her in Jesus' name.
Amen.

Apostle Katherine T. Parker

1

LOVE

Presented by Carolyn W. Scott

"There is no fear in love; but perfect love casteth out fear: because fear hath torment. He that feareth is not made perfect in love." 1 John 4:18 (KJV)

The fruit of the Spirit are the characteristics of God. Love is the main characteristic. Without God's love we can do nothing. The scripture says in 1 John 4:18 (KJV), *"There is no fear in love; but perfect love casteth out fear: because fear hath torment. He that feareth is not made perfect in love."*

There is a song by Tina Turner that asks a question in its title, "What's Love Got to Do with It?" I believe love has a lot to do with it!

In my walk with Christ, I have learned there are different types of love. I believe agape love is the most important. Agape love is unselfish and generous love—the love that God gives us. With agape love, you learn to look beyond each other's faults to see one another's needs. In that, you learn how to be patient with each other. Love gives you the grace to be patient, humble, compassionate, kind, gentle, and meek with everyone. Love teaches you so much. The main thing is that we must humble ourselves and yield our will to the Lord's and allow Him to work in us first.

The Lord does a work on the inside of us first—that inward work. Many times, we do not realize that there is so much on the inside of us that must be cleaned out. When we yield ourselves over to Him and allow Him to work in our lives, He begins to work through us and allows us to be the example to lead others to Christ. It is only through God that we can learn to be patient allowing Him to work on our children, love ones and friends. He wants to use us as an instrument. As the Word says in Ephesians 2:10, we become His workmanship to do the will of God—that is what He is looking for! Workers to do His will! Not our will, but His will be done.

Applying love to our daily living means to be obedient to the Word of God. He said, *"with lovingkindness have I drawn thee"* in Jeremiah 31:3 (KJV). When we yield ourselves and allow God to do work in our hearts, He will show us how to walk in His love. We learn through the Word of God. Not just saying it, but through applying it to our daily lives. Meaning that we must humble ourselves and apply the Word of God.

We can do none of this truly, without salvation. We need to be saved and learn through His Word what it means to be saved. What it means to be saved, is yielding your will to His will and allowing Him to do a new thing in you. You have to want God to work in you. Being prayerful because we have to want to surrender ourselves unto the Lords will. So, we must first realize that we need God—His salvation. In our natural lives, we want to make changes, but the truth is, we can do none of this without the power of God. There are many times, we try to do things in our own lives and it never works until we realize that we need God. Some say "a higher power"—we need Jesus. He is the One who has the power to change the heart of every man—He has the power!

If we can realize that and really want a change, we will yield to His will and embrace salvation. The scriptures in Matthew 11:28-

2

29 (KJV) say, *"Come unto me, all ye that labour and are heavy laden, and I will give you rest. Take my yoke upon you, and learn of me; for I am meek and lowly in heart: and ye shall find rest unto your souls."* We need rest. We're use to trying to do this and do that with in our own power—messing up—so why not trust Jesus? You know we will trust in each other; we will even fail each other! There is NO failure in God!

God's awesome love is that He looks beyond our many faults and sees our needs. God is awesome that his grace and mercies cover us. His grace allows us time to draw near to and grow in Him. Giving us time to make mistakes after we start growing in Him. 1 John 1:9 (KJV), *"If we confess our sins, he is faithful and just to forgive us our sins, and to cleanse us from all unrighteousness."* He is not like man, He forgives us. Confess it, turn away from it, do not look back at it—keep on pressing forward. James 4:7-8 (KJV) admonishes us to "[s]ubmit yourselves therefore to God. Resist the devil, and he will flee from you. Draw nigh to God, and he will draw nigh to you..." In this, God is saying, the more you draw nigh unto me, the enemy will flee from you!

Matthew 5:6 (KJV) says *"[b]lessed are they which do hunger and thirst after righteousness: for they shall be filled."* We must pray and ask God for a hunger and thirst after Him. He is the one working within us. We do know what it is to "hunger" and "thirst," so we need to ask Him. The scripture says in James 4:2 (KJV), "...ye have not, because ye ask not." We can ask God for the things that we desire. We can talk to God and tell Him where we are at and He will show and teach us what to do. The more we yield to Him, the more He will give us. It doesn't matter if we start off small, saying **The Lord's Prayer** in Psalm 23 (KJV):

> *The LORD is my shepherd; I shall not want. ² He maketh me to lie down in green pastures: he leadeth me beside the still*

waters. ³ He restoreth my soul: he leadeth me in the paths of righteousness for his name's sake. ⁴ Yea, though I walk through the valley of the shadow of death, I will fear no evil: for thou art with me; thy rod and thy staff they comfort me. ⁵ Thou preparest a table before me in the presence of mine enemies: thou anointest my head with oil; my cup runneth over. ⁶ Surely goodness and mercy shall follow me all the days of my life: and I will dwell in the house of the LORD forever.

After a while when God sees that He can trust you with that, He will give you some more! The more you yield and run, the more He will give you. He sees the heart of a man. He knows when he is real and not. When you are truly sold out and committed, He can begin to work! It is not all in joining the brick building. He desires your whole heart sold out to Him, meaning that He has captivated you. Once you give Him your heart, He can work on it.

You must go through the process—the inward work. You first go through the mountain of sanctification where He will begin to sanctify you and build you up in His Word. After sanctification comes transformation—God decides to do a work in you. He is the only one who has the power to change the heart of a man who wants to be changed. God is not a God who will force himself on you. You have to want this thing. If he sees your heart, He will do it because He loves you so much.

Love is necessary. To walk in the fruit of the Spirit, God is calling for us to love as He has loved us. God's love is unconditional. Man loves you as longs as you love them the way they want you to or if you are doing the "right" thing that pleases them. The moment you do not they will throw you away, but God's unconditional love means that he loves us despite of the situation or circumstance. While also granting the chance and time to get it together Even in

4

the midst of mistakes, He is right there picking you up and turning you around giving you the constant strength to keep pressing on. He calls for us to look beyond the faults of one another which cannot be done apart from the power of God—His Spirt in us.

Without love we can do nothing. Without His love, everything is in vain. In fact, 1 Corinthians 13:1 (NKJV) says, *"Though I speak with the tongues of men and of angels, but have not love, I have become sounding brass or a clanging cymbal."* When we try to do the work of God without His love, it will not stand. It will fall. We need his love. When we walk in the love of Jesus, we are walking in His anointing. We need the anointed love of God, to do the work of God. We want to be effective and make an awesome impact. Salvation is free, but to walk in His anointing, it cost. It cost to walk in the anointing of God! It is a sacrifice. He does a breaking and deliverance in you to do His will.

The Word of God says in Jeremiah 1:5 (KJV), *"Before I formed thee in the belly I knew thee; and before thou camest forth out of the womb I sanctified thee, and I ordained thee a prophet unto the nations."* I dare you to make it personal and put your name there! He already knew you before you were formed in your mother's womb. He knew you then and surely, He knows you today.

John 3:16 (KJV) goes further sharing that, *"...God so loved the world, that he gave his only begotten Son, that whosoever believeth in him should not perish, but have everlasting life."* This is awesome. God's love towards us is unmerited, we do not deserve it. He is just saying, "come unto me."

Even when I was out in the world, I believed in Jesus Christ, I just did not have a heart relationship with Him. I heard the Word, but I had not yielded, surrendered to it. In fact, I had been hearing it since I was a child but did not yield. Some say that it is not for me, but it is for everybody! Or some say that I am not ready, not ready to give up what they think is peace and joy to stay in mess. Just like in the day of Noah, when he was preparing the Ark, he kept crying out to the people to come on in and they did not harken into the message. Some want to get their last dance, boyfriend, or girlfriend before heeding the call and voice of the Lord. Not realizing that they are rejecting the real joy and love found in Jesus Christ.

It is even more necessary today to draw unto God because people are leaving here left and right. Can you imagine people are going on haven't said, "yes Lord." God is still yet giving us time. We are seeing the power of God even now, in the midst of a world pandemic and societal distress God is speaking, saying "come unto me." While real, our hope and trust should remain in Jesus Christ. The focus is salvation. Getting saved. Having a relationship with God.

When you are in Christ Jesus you are going to see Him again. Everyone thinks they are going to heaven, but you cannot get to heaven until you get your heart right by giving it over to Him. Then He can release His grace, mercy and forgiveness upon you and you can learn to walk in His character.

In order to inherit the Kingdom of God, we must learn to walk in the fruit of the Spirit. The things that will get us closer to the Lord.

Know ye not that the unrighteous shall not inherit the kingdom of God? Be not deceived: neither fornicators, nor idolaters, nor adulterers, nor effeminate, nor abusers of themselves with mankind,10 Nor thieves, nor covetous, nor drunkards, nor revilers, nor extortioners, shall inherit the kingdom of God.11 And such were some of you: but ye are

6

washed, but ye are sanctified, but ye are justified in the name of the Lord Jesus, and by the Spirit of our God.
1 Corinthian 6: 9-11 (KJV)

We need to trust God, not the fruit of evil. We must yield to Him and allow Him to work within us. Even once you are filled with the Holy Ghost, He will not force you. It is a continual process of yielding.

Natural Fruit Comparison

If I would compare the spiritual fruit love with a natural fruit it would be the red apple. The apple symbolizes knowledge, immortality, temptation, fertility, spiritual wisdom, and growth. The apple itself is juicy and offers endless nourishment for the body.

Apples grow with seeds in them. If it is a good apple, it can develop and multiply to produce more good apples. That is when you have a good apple— you can also get an apple that is rotten. Typically, when you get a rotten apple, you do not even think about the seed because you just want to spit it out because it is not good. The apple is like unto our heart, if we have a good heart and take on the love of God, we will draw others to Christ. The more seeds of love we plant the more love we get. Galatians 6:7 (KJV) says, "Be not deceived; God is not mocked: for whatsoever a man soweth, that shall he also reap." We will get all of what we sow with the seeds we sow.

When you plant good fruit, it bears good fruit.

Just as the Word states in Genesis 1:27-29 (NIV) "So God created mankind in his own image, in the image of God he created them; male and female he created them. God blessed them and said to them, "Be fruitful and increase in number; fill the earth and subdue it. Rule over the fish in the sea and the birds in the sky and over every living creature that moves on the ground." Then God said, "I give you every seed-bearing plant on the face of the whole earth and every tree that has fruit with seed in it. They will be yours for food."

Have you ever seen the school pictures of an apple with a worm coming out? In a similar way, we do not want worms to come out of our heart. That is not a sign of a healthy heart or evidence of the love of Jesus working through us.

Personal Reflection

In the natural I have always enjoyed serving others, especially helping them in their time of need or trouble. I have always done this from my heart and allowed it to reflect in my actions. Being kind to others and showing love. For example, I had a gift of sewing. In my family, I was always willing to sew prom gowns and more without murmuring or complaining, many times without cost. God has always embedded that in me. This is one way I know God has used me to show love.

Over the years, God has also showed me how to forgive. Forgive the hurt I went through with my husband, different family members and friends. God taught me how to forgive each one of them and leave them in His hands. He said vengeance is the Lords. We must leave them in God's hands and let Him work on them. I had to remember that John 3:16 included them too. He loved them and died for them to draw closer to Him, as well. We try to do it, but we cannot. It requires Him to fix our hearts and heal us, but again, we need to allow Him to do the work. It is also a process for Him to heal the other person. God is a healer. We must come into the full knowledge of what it means through His Word.

Scriptures to Reflect On

- *"Study to shew thyself approved unto God, a workman that needeth not to be ashamed, rightly dividing the word of truth."*

  2 Timothy 2:15 (KJV)

- *"Howbeit when he, the Spirit of truth, is come, he will guide you into all truth: for he shall not speak of himself; but whatsoever he shall hear, that shall he speak: and he will shew you things to come."*

  John 16: 13 (KJV)

- *"Behold, I stand at the door, and knock: if any man hear my voice, and open the door, I will come in to him, and will sup with him, and he with me."*

  Revelation 3:20 (KJV)

Love went first. It connects with all the fruit. Love had to go first and set the tone because in order to be effective and make an impact we must have the love of God.

Anointed Women of God

2

JOY

Presented by Vonzella Faulk

"...for the joy of the LORD is your strength."
Nehemiah 8:10 (KJV)

Joy is the emotion of great delight or happiness, caused by something delightful, exceptionally good or satisfying. Personally, I believe joy is the source and strength of life. It defeats ill feelings, negativity, and strife. Joy comes from God, who demonstrated in the Garden of Eden, when He created man in his own image. Genesis 1:31 (KJV) says "...God saw everything that he had made, and, behold, it was very good"—with a BIG SMILE.

I can also imagine the expression of the young virgin, Mary, when she experienced the first leap in her womb which was that of "Baby Jesus." As we know it to be, Jesus grew up in a sinful world. But because He loved us so much, He willingly suffered on Calvary's cross as a penalty for our sins. All we had to do was receive. Thank God for Salvation!

Personal Reflection

I can vaguely remember my mother, except that she was kind, loving and could always be found giving to her family, friends, and community. As mom's eighth child, I could often be found in her arms, as she stirred the pot just before mealtime. You can say that I was the "taste-tester." While daddy was working hard—sometimes out of state- to support a family of nine children, momma kept the home intact. As I can remember, momma went to the hospital one day, around about the next day, I heard "momma had a baby," then later the same day received the news that "momma died!" Well this shook my very foundation and changed my life. I was only seven years of age at the time and suddenly without my mother. As you can imagine, I had become so attached to my mother. Things were no longer the same. Through this great loss, God gave our family, my sister Cynthia. I thank God for her— *I love you baby girl!*

From that point, I began to seek the Lord. I did not regret for one moment all that I had experienced at such a tender age. He drew me close to Him and taught me some things that I may have never learned. He taught me love, compassion, generosity, stability, and all that I needed for this journey. Most of all, He gave me joy! *Unspeakable joy!*

Today I am filled with joy because of God working in and through my life. I am filled with joy because of where God has brought me from. He has transitioned me from sinner to saint, out of a place of darkness into the light of life. A sinner saved by grace. Though it seemed that I walked through the valley of death's shadow, "but God!" He let me know that He was right there! God has always been with me. When I could not see a clear path to take, I found out that my heavenly Father was walking with me, all the time. As I imagine seeing only one set of footprints; without a doubt they were the footprints of Jesus. He is the one who carried me, whenever I felt weary and darkness tried to overtake me.

Speaking of A Natural Fruit—Kiwi

My favorite fruit is kiwi and has been for several years. The worth of this fruit is extraordinary. Kiwi is the most nutritional fruit; it is known as a healthy antioxidant grown in the tropics.

Its skin is dark olive and fuzzy. The shape and size are bigger than a jumbo egg. It is referred to as a super fruit because of its nutritional value as it stabilizes our blood pressure and builds our immune system. On the spiritual side it is like the word of God, our Holy Bible has all that we need each day. The substance inside of it takes us to a place in God that our strongest enemy cannot pluck out. Yes, God's word is our nutritional guide. It is all we need to keep focused and flourishing before Him.

"O taste and see that the Lord is good: blessed is the man that trusteth in him." Psalm 34:8 (KJV)

As you move forward on your journey, I admonish you not to ever be afraid of life's experiences. As He has done for me, Jesus will guide you through and teach you ALL that you need to know. It will require you to submit yourself to Him, stay focused, read, and grow in His Word. He will lead you into your destiny, as He already has a plan for your life. Know that this is your day! Now is your time.

No regrets. You shall see His plan unfold in your life! Acknowledge Him, submit, and allow Him to take control. *As the Word says in* Proverbs 3:6 (KJV), *"In all thy ways acknowledge him, and he shall direct thy paths."*

3

PEACE

Presented by Moniette S. Laury

"For I know the thoughts that I think toward you, saith the Lord, thoughts of peace, and not of evil, to give you an expected end." Jeremiah 29:11 (KJV)

Have you ever asked yourself, are you at peace with in? Are you being productive? Or are you even in the right environment to receive? A charged atmosphere, where you can walk in full maturity as the spirit of God nurtures and cultivates you?

~

"I cried out to the Lord, and he answered me from his holy mountain. I lay down and slept, yet I woke up in safety, for the Lord was watching over me."
Psalm 3:4-5 (NLT)

Peace is the product of dependence on God. Sleep never comes easy during a crisis. David had sleepless nights when his son Absalom rebelled and gathered an army to kill him. But he slept peacefully, even during the rebellion. What made the difference? David cried out to the Lord, and the Lord heard him. The assurance of answered prayer brings peace. It is easier to sleep well when we have full assurance that God is in full control of our circumstances. If you are lying awake at night worrying about circumstance you can't change, pour out your heart and soul to God, and thank Him that He is in control. Then sleep will come easier. Trust God all the way for He knows what's best for you.

13

As God ministered to me on this peace journey, He was teaching me how to depend and remain in him. So, he had me to meditate on **The True Vine and The Branches** in John 15:1-8 (NIV).

I am the true vine, and my Father is the gardener. He cuts off every branch in me that bears no fruit, while every branch that does bear fruit he prunes so that it will be even more fruitful. You are already clean because of the word I have spoken to you. Remain in me, as I also remain in you. No branch can bear fruit by itself; it must remain in the vine. Neither can you bear fruit unless you remain in me. "I am the vine; you are the branches. If you remain in me and I in you, you will bear much fruit; apart from me you can do nothing. If you do not remain in me, you are like a branch that is thrown away and withers; such branches are picked up, thrown into the fire and burned. If you remain in me and my words remain in you, ask whatever you wish, and it will be done for you. This is to my Father's glory, that you bear much fruit, showing yourselves to be my disciples.

Keep in mind who you are and your position in Christ, you are the branches. This scripture blessed my mind, body and soul. It taught me how to **position** myself, **equip** myself, gain **access**, **clarity** and walk-in **everlasting** peace, love and joy in Jesus Christ.

Now, Come on in and travel along this peace journey with me...

Position Yourself

"Jesus said to him, "I am the way, and the truth, and the Life; no one comes to the Father but through me." John 14:6 (NKJV)

When you position yourself, you take God's lead by equipping yourself in the Word of God. Being anchored in His Word, shows proof that the seed was planted in good soil—prayer. The fruit was being produced through Godly role models showing spiritual growth through prayer and studying the Word of God.

God literally walked me through this, as He showed me how to position myself by resting in Him to hear from Him. *Let's get right to it!*

My peace journey began on Friday May 31,2019, as midday approached Satan thought he was going to end my life with a hemorrhage stroke. I thank God for my husband's calm, attentive and quick actions as he came straight home and helped save my life. I thought I was walking in my freedom from all the stressful circumstances of life. However, the damage of worrying, stress, and medical conditions literally consumed my body. I loss control and God rescued me from the pressures of life. Little did I know God had another plan for my life. He was preparing me for this journey to walk in peace long before it occurred. The following scripture reminded me of what I needed to do.

Meditate on this:
"Therefore confess your sins to each other and pray for each other so that you may be healed. The prayer of a righteous person is powerful and effective."
James 5:16 (NIV)

God had camped His Angels all around me. My daughter had recorded the move of God as He was saving my life and ministering to me on my bed of healing. My daughter told me as the nurse's were working on me, I was praying, speaking in heavenly language, and singing praise songs. My family and friends joined in with me praying, singing, and trusting God all the way for full recovery.

Meditate on this:
"Rejoice always, pray continually, give thanks in all circumstances; for this is God's will for you in Christ Jesus."
1 Thessalonians 5:16-18 (NIV)

As I reflect over this trial I experienced in life, I have learned to give it all over to God as it was too heavy for me to handle. The peace I walk in at this present time comes from prayer and supplication. God humbled me and taught me through healing and prayer. I give God honor, thanks, and glory for all He has brought me through in life. At times, I needed more from God. This required me to position myself, by means of petition laying before God for direction, healing, rest, wisdom and answered prayer. This helped me remain in and depend on God in every aspect of life.

Equip Yourself
"For we are his workmanship, created in Christ Jesus for good works, which God prepared beforehand, that we should walk in them." Ephesians 2:10 (ESV)

What Is Your Level of Peace—Securely Equipping Yourself

There have been times I wanted to fit in with individuals or with the crowd. Some kind of way, an out of place feeling would come over me letting me know I did not belong. Not knowing or understanding that God was protecting me and equipping me for my future. My grandmother taught my cousins and I how to pray at an early age. I can remember spending weekends at my grandparents' home, where my grandmother would wrap the bottom of her bed with all her grandchildren kneeling on our knees repeating the Lord's prayer. What a wonderful spiritual enrichment for our minds, bodies and souls. I remember that secure foundation helped equip me for life's journey. As I matriculated through elementary, junior and high school I know that it was God who kept me by placing a hedge protection around me.

It is important to know yourself, inside and out; it is only then that you can truly know where you are spiritually. It is in that moment you can ask and answer yourself honestly— "do I have peace?", "how much peace do I have?" If you do not have peace, you are emotionally unstable, making decisions that will not benefit you in life.

When you have a secure relationship with God, you walk in a peace that surpasses all understanding. When you incline your ear and heart to the Holy Spirit, it teaches you how to remain in personal relationship with him. Our personal relationship teaches you how to rest in God, which means cling to Him. Depending on the omnipresence of God to equip you in every area of life giving you access to doors opening through prayer.

God is giving you a safe place to pour out and receive confirmation. Focus on that one thing, the power of God and remembering where your strength comes from. I was aware as a teenager there was something different about me. Every time I thought about doing my own thing, I was convicted. Now keep in mind, I was a young girl seeing some of my peers doing things that young people do. I thought it was cool for me too, until the Holy Spirit rose in me. I did not understand that feeling, but I knew something about that feeling comforted, protected and humbled me. I had a praying mother—every time I looked around, she was laying prostrate, praying for her family. I can recall family and friends would hide and run pass my mother house. They knew if my mother saw them before they reached the bar, on the corner from our house, my mother would start praying over them and they would not make it to the party that night. My mother is a true anointed woman of God. She walks in the Word of God faithfully, so the example of living right was before me daily through my grandmother and mother. Thank You Jesus! I received the Holy Ghost when I was a teenager, the Spirit of God was equipping and teaching me how to pray in my heavenly language. My God, I knew then that prayer absolutely changes things as it was evident in my life. Prayer kept me from falling into the enemies' pit.

Access
"In whom we have boldness and access with confidence through faith in Him." Ephesians 3:12 (NKJV)

Having access to the things of God is a humbling experience. Just close your eyes, relax, trusting God for everything, and walking confidently in Him. Now you are walking by faith and confidently in the abundance of God. By gaining immediate access to God through Christ, you can approach Him without an elaborate system. Our privileges are significant with our new life in Christ. We may grow in faith, overcoming doubts and questions and deepening our relationship with God. We can enjoy encouraging one another and worshipping together.

The welcome mat is rolled out with acceptance and availability.

> *And so, dear brothers and sisters, we can boldly enter heaven's Most Holy Place because of the blood of Jesus. By his death, Jesus opened a new and life-giving way through the curtain into the Most Holy Place. And since we have a great High Priest who rules over God's house, let us go right into the presence of God with sincere hearts fully trusting*

him. For our guilty consciences have been sprinkled with Christ's blood to make us clean, and our bodies have been washed with pure water.

Hebrews 10:19-22 (NLT)

Clarity

Meditate on this:
"Before I formed thee in the belly I knew thee; and before thou camest forth out of the womb I sanctified thee, and I ordained thee a prophet unto the nations."

Jeremiah 1:5 (NKJV)

God knows your beginning and end. You are a Jewel; know your worth. The turbulence in your life has settled down and disappeared. It's time for you to throw your weight around in the spirit, to let the enemy know you have arrived. Walk fully and confidently in the fruit of the Spirit, leaving the runway clear for take-off. The time has come for you to dig deeper, flow in your calling as God has called you.

"For I know the thoughts that I think toward you, saith the Lord, thoughts of peace, and not of evil, to give you an expected end." Jeremiah 29:11 (KJV)

Everlasting

"When the Lord takes pleasure in any one's way, he causes their enemies to make peace with them." Proverbs 16:7 (NIV)

God has fully prepared and equipped you for your peace journey. You can flow in a fresh anointing from God with His everlasting peace, love, kindness and protection.

Knowing the many roles or titles we carry, are you fulfilling the call God has placed over your life? We wear many hats, it is wise to concentrate on one thing at a time. Let God do the work in you, rest and be at peace. Walk in peace, love, and joy.

To walk-in everlasting peace, love, and joy in Jesus Christ, you must know the value of your "food grade."

What is your food grade?

The term, "food grade," refers to the materials used in equipment. To be defined as food grade, materials need to be non-toxic and safe for consumption. For your fruit production, know your fruit grades do not use low quality soil or materials. This in mind, let us look at food grade of natural fruit and spiritual fruit.

When comparing the food grade of the natural fruit and spiritual fruit, we must observe the natural man and the spirit man of an individual. So, let us compare the orange in the natural. We would find that the orange is a citrus fruit that grows through a process called germination where the orange seed is sown into moist soil to begin growth. This process produces a seedling of the orange seed which grows into a tree and in time, the tree bears flowers and the flowers produce the fruit with seed. The Orange has an oval shape covered in a tough outer rind which opens to an inner rind that's white, spongy, and non-aromatic. When the orange is ripe, it has an orange or yellow coloring with a sweet taste. On the other hand, let us observe peace, one of the fruit of the Spirit. Peace in the Spirit is an inner sense of serenity, harmony, wholeness, completeness, security, success and well-being.

Depending on your personal emotions and behavior one's attitude may go through the various fruits of the orange family from bitter to sweet. In this case, one's inner man needs nurturing and strength from the spiritual fruit to bring inner peace to calm the natural man down, showing him the purpose for his being. Here we see the individual must make a conscious decision on one's relationship in Jesus Christ, will it be personal or not?

Your Peace Action Plan

A. Speak and Post Affirmations Daily
I walk in Peace
I walk in Harmony
I walk in God's Confidence
I am in Position
I am Love
I am Free
I am Fruitful
I am Successful

B. Walk By Faith In The Word

Hebrew 11:1 (KJV)—"Now faith is the substance of things hoped for, the evidence of things not seen."

Philippians 4:9 (NIV)— "Whatever you have learned or received or heard from me, or seen in me-put it into practice. And the God of peace will be with you."

C. Allow God to take full control of your life
When God is in full control of your life you can make a deposit and immediately withdraw from it. *Walk by faith, not by sight.*

D. Receive God's peace through the wind of the Holy Spirit
God is giving you fresh wind; it is time to walk in your *new* peace in the fruit of the Spirit!

What is your new peace? Name it.
What does fresh wind mean to you? Define it.
What is the result of answered prayer to you?
Declare and Decree it.

E. Inner Peace

This peace I have, the world did not give it to me, and the world cannot take it away. I gained direct access through the power of God.

F. Self-Care

- Know your self-worth.
- Do not cheapen yourself.
- You are valuable.
- Your quiet place is your rich place.
- I will be by myself not to lose myself.

G. Word Knowledge

- **Position**— a particular way someone or is placed or arranged (posture, stance, attitude)
- **Equip**— prepare (someone) mentally for a particular situation or task (prepare, provide, qualify, endow)
- **Access**— a means of approaching or entering in a place (entry, entrance, way in, gain access)
- **Clarity**— quality of being coherent and intelligible (simplicity, plainness, precision)
- **Everlasting**— lasting a long time or a very long time (endless, never ending, eternal)
- **Inner Peace**— refers to a state of being mentally or spiritually at peace. To have enough knowledge and strength for oneself to face discord or stress.

- **Peace in the Natural**— a calm, quiet time without fight, war or disturbances

In conclusion, bearing the fruit of the Spirit represents the nature of God's Spirit. It shows evidence of the Holy Spirit dwelling within you. As you walk in the Spirit of God bearing the fruit of the Spirit will nurture, cultivate, and mature you for your spirit filled journey.

Think on these words, *"Do not be conformed to this world, but be transformed by the renewal of your mind, that by testing you may discern what is the will of God, What is good and acceptable and perfect."* Romans 12:2 (ESV)

As you move on this peace journey, flow in harmony, serenity, integrity, love, and peace. Think on the peace of God through scripture.

Walk in your peace journey immediately.
Your fruit production is overflowing!

4

LONGSUFFERING

Presented by Carla B. Scott

"And we know that all things work together for good to them that love God, to them who are the called according to his purpose." Romans 8:28 (KJV)

Sometimes there are going to be invitations that you cannot deny. And the day of the Fruit of the Spirit Fellowship was one of those invitations. The person who asked me to be apart happens to have birthed me and she has endured so much with and for me. So, nothing could keep me from being present to share that day.

My fruit is "**longsuffering,**" not knowing that I would have endured so much the weeks prior leading up to sharing my portion. My muse was my sister.... The Webster's Dictionary definition for longsuffering started off as "patiently enduring lasting offense or hardship"—let that sink in. Then I looked up the word patiently in the same source and it stated in a manner with calmness, without complaint or hurry, despite of delays and or difficulties, etc. meaning we can go on and on and on with examples.

Today what I want to urge and challenge you with is this, none of us are exempt from life's challenges, experiences, or anything. It does not matter if you are homeless, pastor, president, or the pope. You are never going to be exempt from not experiencing the hand of cards life deals you. So, we must set our lives up accordingly to be able to endure and be sustained by God when Life decides to show up and show out.

I was living in Charlotte, North Carolina in May of 2019 when I received a call from the family in Baltimore informing me that my sister had a stroke and there was bleeding on her brain. This was after she had a previous visit to the emergency room for a headache and was sent home to later be found home by her husband in the floor in excruciating pain. I immediately booked my travel plans to get to Baltimore as soon as possible. In the midst of all of that, she was taken to another hospital in Washington DC due to her condition to be further treated by the neurological team.

I traveled by Mega Bus to DC, caught the local bus to the area of the hospital and from there a cab to the main entrance of the hospital. Needless to say, my nerves were plucked at that point. When I saw my sister in that hospital bed it was not her normal look and my heart was broken. So, as we were waiting for them to do the surgery to release the pressure on her brain from the bleed, we received the report that the bleeding had stopped—let me pause here and say God is awesome! All I know is surgery was no longer needed and God was starting that healing process right then.

When my mother asked me what fruit I felt best fit me, I said longsuffering because it was evident, He was teaching and showing me this particular fruit. When you are going through you must know who your guide and navigator is and what will get you through the rough times. It is easy to get distracted and worry about what others may think of you and your life decisions. You must develop a "Mind Your Business" mentality, in a positive way, to cancel out any negative energy and vibes when you are fighting to get through life challenges and storms.

If I would compare longsuffering to a natural fruit, it would be a "pomegranate." Pomegranate was one of my favorite fruits. Although it could be messy and stain everything, it was well worth it after enduring the process of getting into the inside and tasting the sweet juices. Pomegranate has a hard, husky outer skin and a soft membrane feel on the inside with several buds of juice. The way it is designed is so unique and some would say it is too much, too messy, or just not worth the time to indulge. Likewise, in life, you are going to have to encounter and deal with some unique situations that will not necessarily make sense or feel good when you are going through them. The more you push through, not worrying about what your situation looks like, it allows you to focus more on enduring and coming out of it with the best outcome possible. It will not only mature you physically, but also spiritually and heighten your ability to weather the next storm, trial and situation that may occur thereafter in your life. Only the strong will survive.

The question to ask is, who is the source of your strength when you are weak? Who gives you joy in times of sorrow? Who picks you up when you fall? What drives you when it seems like all hope is lost? My God will always carry you through whatever comes your way whenever you let him take control of your life.

You must read the word to the end and speak it into your life. It is scriptures like *"... **weeping may endure for a night, but joy cometh in the morning**" **Psalm 30:5, KJV.** Do not stop reading and/or get stuck at weeping and enduring but press through to the joy in the morning. We do not have time to let other people and their opinions weigh so heavily on how we are moving and operating in our lives and our decision making. Understand that whatever we go through and how we come out is a direct reflection to our legacy and lineage.

So, in everything get an understanding, focus, stay the course, pray without ceasing, affirm yourself, encourage yourself, keep positive energy flowing in your midst, meditate, self-evaluate, be inspired, and aspire for greatness. All these things will cultivate your life and sustain you along the journey to triumph.

5

KINDNESS

Presented by Mone't S. Horton

"And whatever you do, in word or deed, do everything in the name of the Lord Jesus, giving thanks to God the Father through him." Colossians 3:17 (ESV)

When I think of the fruit of the spirit kindness, I think about the scripture, *"... I have loved thee with an everlasting love: therefore with lovingkindness have I drawn you"* **Jeremiah 31:3, KJV.** Here we see that kindness was not by itself, rather it was coupled with love. I also think about the saying that is often quoted, "people will forget about what you said, but they will never forget about how you made them feel." So, I would define kindness as going beyond one's self, showing through action, generosity and pure love. Also making yourself friendly—the Word of God also talks about showing yourself friendly, while cautioning us to wisely select.

Proverbs 18:24 (ESV)
A man of many companions may come to ruin, but there is a friend who sticks closer than a brother.
Proverbs 27:9 (ESV)
Oil and perfume make the heart glad, and the sweetness of a friend comes from his earnest counsel.
Matthew 22:39 (ESV)
And a second is like it: You shall love your neighbor as yourself.
Luke 6:31 (ESV)
And as you wish that others would do to you, do so to them.

That is the only way that you can make friends or begin to tap into those commonalities you may have with another person even within another community, church, work, school or while out shopping.

Kindness is going beyond yourself. In reflecting on the scriptures, I see that God has always been found going beyond himself and thinking about others. There is a saying, "What Would Jesus Do." When I think about myself, while I do not see myself as a mean and negative person, sometimes I know that kindness is not always at the forefront of my thoughts. Being human, kindness is not always on the forefront of our mind, think intently on what God would do and how can I put someone else's needs or desires before my own in any given situation. If we are honest, that is not always the case. I believe that is what God does and continues to do, in terms of us. When I sit and think on the times that I did not follow Gods direction and I did not follow the principles, standards that he laid before me in His Word. If he was not kind to me, then where would I be today? He has always shown His generosity and He calls me friend. In spite of us, in spite of our downfalls and not following instructions He still calls us friend. That is kindness—showing through His actions how much He loves us.

John 15:15 (NIV)
I no longer call you servants, because a servant does not know his master's business. Instead, I have called you friends, for everything that I learned from my Father I have made known to you.
He draws me (us) with His love and kindness.

In that same vein, if we are to be examples of God in the earth then we are to also show kindness, love, tender mercies to other people. Not that they are not in the wrong, but because the Word

29

of God says so. The Word calls for us to be KIND; calls for us to think of someone more highly than ourselves. It calls us to think what would Jesus do in this situation—would He blow up, puff up, get upset or would He step back, take evaluation of the situation to see how He could take the high road as opposed to the low one. How can He make an impact?

Proverbs 3:28 (ESV)
Do not say to your neighbor, "Go, and come again, tomorrow I will give it"—when you have it with you.
1 Corinthians 13:4 (ESV)
Love is patient and kind; love does not envy or boast; it is not arrogant

This in mind, there is still a delicate balance when showing kindness because sometimes we can use these characteristics to our detriment. While God calls us to be kind, he also calls us to exercise a level of wisdom, even when we do not understand. It is important because if we only look at the fact that yes God is calling us to be generous , show ourselves friendly, we may cause ourselves to become overwhelmed and overexerted because we are being people pleasers—trying to win them to our side. That is NOT what God has called us to do. He is calling us to be a people who is in alignment with His will and His plan and in doing so, that does not mean that we always have to say YES, YES, YES. I recall listening to Bishop TD Jakes' sermon one day and he said, "you have to embrace the NO." I had to begin to incorporate this in my life and my walk with Christ. I am learning that there is power in the "NO." So, being kind does not always mean, yes, yes, yes, but what it does mean is that the same grace, generosity, love and kindness that God has given me, I must pour out to others while exercising wisdom.

He has called us to be wise. He does not want us to operate out of burnout, being overwhelmed or overextended. No, no, no. There are several ways that we can show kindness in the world today. For an example, today we have what they call "acts of kindness." People show in different ways every day. In many ways it causes us to be focused and aware of where we are putting our energies—are we focusing on us? Is it a "selfie"? Am I being selfish or selfless? Asking myself these questions, helps me to take the focus off me and place it on the needs of others. I do not have to know your whole life situation or what you have in your bank account right now, or your gas tank right now, but I am going to think about you. Kindness does not have a dollar sign on it. It does not mean that you must spend a lot of money on it in order to make a world of a difference in someone's life. Just to know that, oh you thought about me today. You did not have to, but you did. You did not just think about yourself, you included me in that, and for that I am thankful. So, kindness is taking the spotlight off you and putting it on someone else. Taking your own resources and giving them to someone else. When we do that, we can always count on living in a place of overflow. When we give to others unselfishly, we can always count on Gods blessings in our lives. God blesses those who bless, give and give out of the gratitude of their heart. It is the intent that is important. That is why it is important for the believer to operate out of a place of kindness.

Personal Testimony & Reflections

As a young adult I recall spending so much time and energies in church, with the youth and young adult ministry. Having such a desire to mentor and build up young people and help others. I did so much and in the end, I felt like I was being taken for granted. As I reflect, I must check my intent—did I do it for someone to recognize me or praise? No, I can say that I did it to

31

do God's will and fill the burning desire with in to help someone else. When I look back over my life, I am where I am today because someone took the time to mentor me, pour into me, take a moment of their time to support me—they showed me one act of kindness after another. Someone may have put a good word in for me, looked out for me, went out on the limb for me. Today, I have a burning desire to help other people. Fuel their fire, help push them into their destiny and purpose for being here on earth. The bad and painful experiences that I have had in the past were fueled by family and those closest to me.

I am fueled and I know what God has placed inside of me. I know that if it wasn't for His grace and mercy I would not be here today. I refuse to allow my past experiences to impact me moving forward to make a difference in the lives of those He has placed in my way. I do not want to go and then stop, go and then STOP! That is the life I do not want to live. I want to be consistently in action moving toward fulfilling God's purpose for my life. No, it is not easy, but it challenges me even the more to intentionally look for opportunities to get out of my own way and do something for someone else. Big or small.

- ☐ I do not want to be labeled as "busy" rather I want to be productively walking out my purpose.
- ☐ I will surrender me and go after the things that God has me to do on this earth.
- ☐ I do not want to wait, I do not want to pause
- ☐ I want to go after it with everything in me—with all my being!
- ☐ I do not want to sit on the side lines.
- ☐ I want to be vulnerable—I am willing to be vulnerable to breakthrough!

I am not perfect, but really do have a heart to serve. I just do not like when individuals take your kindness for weakness or take advantage of you! It is NOT a good feeling! I know that God felt it ALL, yet HE still LOVED! Even in the midst of it all and that is what He wants Us to do! God continued to pour out while receiving nothing in return, He remained in a place of service. Showing acts of kindness, wherever He went. What a perfect example?! So, kindness is and must be intentional. Meaning that it requires an exerted effort to act and perform towards an intended result.

Romans 5:8 (ESV)
But God shows his love for us in that while we were still sinners, Christ died for us.

For example, with me I can be so focused on getting the job done and getting to the end result and resolve the situation that I do not see all of the opportunities and ways (to max out) that I could have extended kindness in THAT MOMENT. Beyond a hug, beyond a word—as the saying goes, "people will forget what you said, but they will never forget how you made them feel." How am I making people feel daily? Do I have kind communication? How was my facial expression? My tone? –this is all so real to me! In that moment, you have an awesome opportunity to be a light in showing kindness.

Kindness like a Watermelon[1]

When I think about how kindness should flow throughout our lives it puts me in the mind of the natural fruit, watermelon. There are two (2) main types of watermelon—seedless and

---

[1] U.S. Department of Agriculture (USDA) Library. 2020. <https://www.nal.usda.gov/fnic/melons> and National Watermelon Promotion Board. 2020. <www.Watermelon.org>

seeded. You would not know this from viewing them on the outside because they look the same. In research, I learned that seedless watermelons have little to no black seeds, if any, but they still contain white seed coats that represent the seeds that did not mature. I further learned that seedless melons do not produce enough pollen, so they need seeded melon in order to pollinate and generate more fruit. In addition, farmers usually must go a step farther in placing beehives in their fields to encourage reproduction and cultivation between the seeded and seedless plants. On the other hand, seeded watermelons can stand alone, they are authentic to the core with seeds that are mature and can keep producing! When you cut open a seeded melon you see the black seeds embedded throughout the red flesh of the melon, they are not concentrated in one area. This was so interesting to me and made me think, this is the way kindness should flow through our lives. Kindness should be sprinkled throughout our lives.

I see kindness, or what has been coined "acts of kindness" as these watermelon seeds that should be planted in the lives of others, we encounter for the purpose of spreading love and compassion throughout the world. Now, we never know the total impact of our seeds of kindness, but we do have a responsibility to intentionally plant. Like the seeded melon, sometimes our ability to show kindness can cause someone who lacks the maturity to change his/her ways or mindset that can make a greater impact in his/her life and those connected to them. Wow—there is power in the seed!

Let us go beyond the seed! While the watermelon is typically enjoyed when sliced, juiced, chilled or grilled and served during the summer months it should not be limited because it can be enjoyed all year long. Watermelon offers a wealth of health benefits containing several vitamins (A, C, B6), minerals and dietary fiber that contribute to healthy living. Also 92% of the watermelon fruit itself is made up of water and our bodies need water to survive. A few documented health benefits of watermelon include, but are not limited to the following:

- *Aids in hydration*
- *Boost immune system*
- *Promotes weight loss*
- *Improves eyesight*
- *Helps to maintain healthy skin and hair*
- *Produces energy*
- *Reduces high blood pressure and blood sugar levels*

- *Reduces Heart Disease*
- *Reduces risk and fights against some types of cancer*
- *Improves circulation*
- *Soothes muscle soreness*
- *A powerful antioxidant*
- *Maintains kidney health*

Like watermelon, kindness cannot and should not be bound to just one function, season or time period. Kindnesses ability to reproduce can far exceed our expectations if we just accept the responsibility and embrace the opportunity to plant the seed. When we exercise kindness, we live life at another level and access all the bountiful blessings that God has always made available to us.

Learning about the watermelon has been refreshing to me! The watermelons peel (the outer green layer) can be carved adding style to any table, gathering, event or exhibit—a work of art, a masterpiece. The rind (inner layer between the red flesh and outer layer) can be used for pickles, slaw etc. elevating and adding flavor to any dish. The seeds can be roasted used to compliment any salad or meal. This means that 100% of the watermelon can be used in one shape or another. It is literally up to our disposal—how many times have you thrown away any of these components of the watermelon?

In the same token, **kindness perpetuates.** There is another saying "paying it forward"—when I do one kind thing, take on a burden or lift a weight off of someone else it gives them space and room to maybe do something for someone else. Then it continues, going and going and going. So many times, it goes beyond the day, the week, month and year. It just continues into time. So, we never want to minimize our seed (act) of kindness just to that moment. **Kindness goes on and can evolve into a masterpiece, a movement that can change the trajectory of a life, a relationship, a family, a community and even a nation.**

Today, I want you to think about how many times you missed out on an opportunity to plant a seed of kindness? Now, you have an opportunity to make a difference moving forward. How you can plant seeds of kindness in someone else's life? How can you perpetuate, pass it on, literally change someone's day, by planting a seed of kindness? How far will your kindness go? Will it be far reaching, exceeding your intent and expectation?

We can never know the full impact of our seeds of kindness, but as the word of God says in 1 Corinthians 3:6 AMP, *"I planted, Apollos watered, but God [all the while] was causing the growth."* Meaning, we all have a role, we may be the planter one day and maybe the waterer another day, but in either case we must play our part and look to God to make the increase. He always holds up His end! We must not grow tired, weary, weak, fickle or worn when it comes to doing that which is right. Galatians 6:9 admonishes us to hold on saying, "Let us not grow weary or become discouraged in doing good, for at the proper time we will reap, if we do not give in."

I am grateful for the opportunity given to really meditate on kindness and how I can reinforce its presence more in my life. It made me realize that I should never allow someone else's response or actions impact my responsibility and obligation on earth as an ambassador of the Kingdom of God. I will show kindness because I know, like the watermelon, every aspect of it, whether it is the seed, the rind, the peel or the red flesh, it can be used. Whether someone uses it to create something even more beautiful, to sprinkle it or in the moment to enjoy a cool and refreshing desert or that seed of kindness can be roasted and marinated over time to give birth to even more seeds of kindness. It does not matter, but choose today to allow kindness to flow through your life.

Allow kindness to disrupt your routine. When it does, find the strength and courage to proceed forward without hesitation or delay. There you will find the bountiful graces that cause you to excel beyond what you can ever imagine. Allow kindness to WIN!

1 Chronicles 16:11 (ESV)
Seek the LORD and his strength; seek his presence continually!

Action Work –Personal Evaluation

Evaluate—
What are ways that you have tried to draw people? Persuade them to see something from your side, your point of view? What are ways that you recall someone trying to draw or persuade you? Did you feel it was genuine? Was it "from the heart?" What is kind? Did you feel that there was a posture of kindness or did they do it just to check off that they did it?

Demonstrate—
Think about how you can demonstrate kindness, show an act of kindness today. What you would like someone to do for you. Remember that act, which made a world of a difference in someone's life. That would put a smile on their face.

Before you even open your mouth, what are you saying? What is your posture, demeanor, behavior saying/showing about you? And when you open your mouth—what are you saying? Where are your words coming from? Is it kind communication? What is your word choice? What is the impact of your words?

Elevate–
I charge you today and every-day to make a continuous decision to be kind—to show yourself friendly. Rise above you—your feelings and emotions.

A Prayer of Intentional Kindness

God, I pray right now, that you would help me to get it right.
I want to really get into me and out of me at the same time.
Help me to focus on the things that really matter.
Help me to show love and kindness in every opportunity provided.
I want to be totally in it with you without hesitation.
Help me to show love and kindness that extends beyond me.
Help me to stay focused and connected.
In this time of uncertainty, help me to go deep within and find the strength to reach out and respond to the needs of others around me to make an impact!
I need you to show me how to do this Oh Lord!
To do your will, I pray.
God, I thank and praise you in this moment.
I give you ALL glory and honor.
Father, I trust you.
I will lean not unto my own understanding, but acknowledge you in all my ways, so that you will continue to direct my path.
I will trust you even when I cannot trace you or even when I do not understand. Help me to be a better me.
Show me how to be kind; not paralyzed by my past, rather to be patient and prayerful towards your purpose and plan.
Thank you, Lord, for this journey! This journey that is making me better.
In Jesus' name, Amen.

Mone't S. Horton

6

GOODNESS

Presented by Jacqueline Ejim

"O taste and see that the Lord is good: blessed is the man that trusteth in him." Psalm 34:8 (KJV)

Galatians 5:22-23 (NKJV) outlines the spiritual fruit the Holy Spirit produces in our lives, so that we can positively impact the body of Christ and world. I invite you on this journey as I share on the spiritual fruit, goodness.

The dictionary defines goodness as kindness, generosity or beneficial. The Greek word for goodness is "agathosune," which means zeal for truth and righteousness and a hatred of evil; it can be expressed in acts of kindness (Luke 7:37-50) or in rebuking and correcting evil (Matthew 21:12-13)[2].

When I think of the spiritual fruit goodness, I think of the natural fruit mango. Mangos have a sweet flavor, tastes good, and deliver a host of nutrients that are beneficial to the natural body. They contain over 20 different vitamins and minerals, helping to make them a super food.

Externally, mangos are multi-colored, often varying in red, yellow, and green colors. In comparison, the spiritual fruit of goodness, is not restricted to any set culture or people. Goodness is accessible to all, no matter which ethnic background or person.

---

[2]KJV Life in the Spirit Study Bible; Galatians 5:22, Ephesians 5:9. 1992, 2003, by Life Publishers International

At times, they can be found battered, bruised, and torn; however, in this state, valuable nutrients can still be found on the inside. Similarly, there are people who have been misused, battered, bruised, and torn; they feel as though there is no good thing that can come from their lives. However, that is so far from the truth! No matter what it may feel like and or look like, they are valuable both inside and out.

When one consumes a mango, he/she can take part in the awesome taste and experience goodness in his/her health. Some immediate benefits of mangos include, but are not limited to, prevention of cancer, lower cholesterol, clear the skin, improve eye health, alkalize the whole body, improve digestion, fight heat stroke and boost the immune system.

Likewise, walking in the fruit of the Spirit, enables one to taste and see the goodness of the Lord. When walking in the goodness of God, one can focus on living in accordance with His will. This alone can empower one to live in purity, by omitting sexual immorality, not yielding to lustful pleasures, idolatry, sorcery, hostility, quarreling, jealousy, outbursts of anger, selfish ambition, dissension, division, envy, drunkenness, wild parties, and other ungodly behaviors (disobedience to God) that interfere with doing God's will.

When we act out of true goodness of heart, we are obedient to God's commandments and seek the well-being of others, not ourselves. We truly care for and seek the highest good of another person without motive of personal gain. For example, volunteering to serve meals at a homeless shelter is a way that we can seek to put others needs before our own and show God's goodness.

God's goodness conveys His generosity. His goodness means far more than His generosity, but it generally includes His infinitely generous attitude toward us. By nature, He longs to bring joy and blessing to all His creatures.

We can affirm the goodness of God through the Names of God, for example:
- *Elohim God, Creator Mighty and Strong (Genesis 17:7; Genesis 1:1)*
- *El-Shaddai Almighty God who is sufficient and all bountiful (Genesis 49:24; Psalm 132:2,5)*
- *Adonai Excellent in all the earth (Genesis 15:2; Judges 6:15)*
- *Jehovah Jireh our provider (Genesis 22:14)*
- *Jehovah Raphe Healer (Exodus 15:26)*
- *Jehovah Shalom the Lord is Peace (Judges 6:24)*

God loves us so much. In the beginning he created a perfect world full of good things, no sickness or death. He called everything He made "good" but called man "very good." When man disobeyed God, disobedience caused a separation between God and humankind. God loved humankind so much; more than anything, so, He sent His only begotten son, Jesus, as an advocate to pay for our sins and redeem us so we can be close to God again.

Jesus, the Son of God, was a great example for humanity. He could always be found going about doing good throughout His travels. In fact, He went to a party turned water into wine, fed 5000 hungry people with 5 loaves of bread and 2 fish, calmed a raging storm by telling it to stop, walked on water, He healed sick people, healed the blind to see, healed the paralyzed to walk, touched sick diseases, raised the dead, forgave sins and healed on the inside. Likewise, as children of God, we are commissioned to go about doing good in Jesus name confident that miracles signs and wonders shall follow us as long as we move in accordance with God's will.

Personal Testimony

I thank God for an opportunity to share a portion of my testimony on how the Holy Spirit (Power of God) enabled me to demonstrate walking in the fruit of the Spirit, goodness.

I am the youngest of eight siblings. My mother reared us in a single parent household in the inner city. All of my siblings suffered with alcohol and drug addictions except for my oldest sister and myself. After living a dysfunctional life of sexual immorality, impurity, lustful pleasures, idolatry, sorcery , hostility, quarreling, jealousy, outbursts of anger, selfish ambition , dissension, division, envy, drunkenness, wild parties, and other ungodly behaviors (disobedience to God); the goodness of God changed my life.

In the year 1987, I met a young man who made a great impact in my life. This young man was peculiar, and he was anointed by God. He introduced me to God, church and showed me another way of living. During this time, I accepted Jesus Christ as my personal Lord and Savior. The Holy Spirit taught me how to live a meaningful and purpose filled life that is pleasing to God. In 1992, we were joined in Holy Matrimony and I inherited two wonderful step- children. Through this union and inheritance, I have learned the importance of placing faith (God) first, family second and finances third on my priority list. In 1990, I met a young lady who was a Pastor and became my spiritual mentor. This Pastor was rooted and grounded in Christianity and she was an excellent example of a Christian. She not only preached the Word of God, but she also lived her life according to the Word of God. She taught me how to pray, fast and stand still to wait on

God for an answer. In addition, she taught me how to study the Word of God and search the scriptures to find answers. Today, I am able to live according to the Word of God because of her teachings and illustrations.

After being married over 25 years, my husband chose to live a life of sexual immorality, impurity, lustful pleasures, and other ungodly behaviors that attempted to lure me back into that lifestyle; but after tasting of the goodness of the Lord ; I chose to stay connected to God, to continue with the goodness of the Lord. It was a very painful process leaving because I vowed to be a lifetime partner. Initially, I loved my ex-husband soooo much that I did almost anything and everything to please him. Later, I began to feel convictions of God and became so Godly sorry about the things that God had delivered me from. Sometimes it seemed as though I was going to lose my mind. It felt like my mind was slipping and I was going to lose control of my life. I could not sleep, eat, or work. I could not do anything but cry. I began to pray scriptures: Isaiah 6:23 reminding the Lord that he promised to keep me in perfect peace whose mind is stayed on him because I trusted him. I also prayed 2 Timothy 1:7 thanking God for not giving me a spirit of fear but of power, love and a sound mind. Additionally, I kept applying the Power of the Blood of Jesus over my mind.

I thank and praise God; He gave me a breakthrough instead of a breakdown. During my transition of severing all ungodly ties from my ex-husband and his girlfriend, I had authority and power to leave with everything that we acquired during our marriage. Many tried to persuade me to evict my ex-husband and his girlfriend, sell my house and let him be homeless. God reminded me that it was because of the Goodness of God and Gods' unconditional love for us that He sent His only begotten Son Jesus Christ to restore us all back unto God; and how Jesus went about doing good. Therefore, I was compelled to stay with God on the good path of life. As I journey on, my prayer is that God help us to do what is good, what God wants us to do. Knowing that the good life in God's eyes is for us to act justly, to love mercy and to walk humbly before God. I pray God give us the courage, grace and strength to do what God will have us to do. I look to God and walk on. I love living the good life with the Lord. The Lord impressed on my heart to share half of the money with my ex-husband and to only do good / no harm to my ex-husband. Therefore, I was compelled to obey God. As I remember reading the scripture Luke 23:33-34 as Jesus was crucified, yet He kept doing good; saying "Father forgive them for they know not what they do." In Genesis 45: 1-5 and Genesis 50:20 Joseph continued to do good even when his brothers sold him in Egypt, saying, "But as for you ,ye thought evil against me: but God meant it unto good, to bring to pass, as it is this day, to save much people alive."

I thank and praise the Lord for his mighty acts and his wondrous works! As I reflect over my life, I can see the hand of God and his goodness throughout my life. It is God that has always been there, leading me, guiding me and protecting me. Today my family is blessed! We have all been set free through the blood I of Jesus Christ Our Lord and Savior! God has blessed me with a new husband, and we walk together in the Lord!

Sometimes life happens and the cares of this world can cause one to forget the Goodness of the Lord, lose love for one another, and to become mean and unkind. This is a plea, do not let the cares of this world cause you to forget the goodness of the Lord and cause you to become mean, unloving, and unkind toward others. Romans 12:2 says, "Be not conformed to this world but be ye transformed by the renewing of your mind, that ye may prove what is that good, and acceptable, and perfect will of God."

In order to walk in the goodness of the Lord, accept Jesus Christ as your personal Lord and Savior (Romans 10:10; 10:13). Pray, read and surrender to the Word of God. Apply the Word of God to your life daily, continue to stay connected to God and allow God's goodness to continue to flow from the inside!

7

FAITHFULLNESS

Presented by

Euphrasynia Love Cookley

"Understand, therefore, that the Lord your God is indeed God. He is the faithful God who keeps his covenant for a thousand generations and lavishes his unfailing love on those who love him and obey his commands."
Deuteronomy 7:9 (NLT)

The dictionary definition of faithful is loyal, steadfast and constant. When I think of faithfulness, I can't help but to think of unfaithfulness, (untrue, fickle and inconstant) in a natural manner. As women, when we are in a marriage or courtship, we desire a faithful man. We expect our husband or companion to be faithful to us. We want and should be the only woman he gives gifts to, the only one he spends quality time with, shares his most private thoughts, hopes and dreams with, and most definitely the only one he is romantic and intimate with. The covenant relationship should be honored and respected with faithfulness. Unfortunately, some woman have experienced being with an unfaithful husband or partner. Let's be real about it. Whether we credit, the Holy Spirit or women's intuition we know when something isn't right. In most cases, we began to investigate via checking his cell phone, email, pants pockets, wallet and everywhere else we can look for proof to confirm our suspicion. If we find proof, it is both hurtful and devastating to know that un-faithfulness resides where faithfulness should live. Knowing or imagining how this experience would make us feel in the natural, why are we satisfied with being unfaithful to a faithful God?

The Lord our God is faithful. When we say God is faithful, it means He is totally trustworthy. It means every covenant He makes; He will keep. It means He will fulfill every unconditional promise He made and according to Hebrews 6:18, it is impossible for God to lie. The faithfulness of God is His attribute that displays His trustworthiness based on His unwavering commitment to His people through His promises and covenants that find their ultimate fulfillment in the person of Jesus Christ. I invite you to discover His faithfulness through accepting Him as your personal savior, through relationship and reading His Word.

- 1 Corinthians 1:9 (CSB)— "God is faithful; you were called by Him into fellowship with His Son, Jesus Christ our Lord."

- 1 Corinthians 10:13 (CSB)— "No temptation has come upon you except what is common to humanity. But God is faithful; he will not allow you to be tempted beyond what you are able, but with the temptation he will also provide the way out so that you may be able to bear it."

- 2 Thessalonians 3:3 (NIV)— "But the Lord is faithful, and he will strengthen you and protect you from the evil one."

- Numbers 23:19 (NLT)—"God is not a man, so he does not lie. He is not human, so he does not change his mind. Has he ever spoken and failed to act? Has he ever promised and not carried it through?"

- 1 John 1:9 (NLT)— "But if we confess our sins to him, he is faithful and just to forgive us our sins and to cleanse us from all wickedness."

- Hebrews 11:11(NASB)— "By faith even Sarah herself received ability to conceive, even beyond the proper time of life, since she considered Him faithful who had promised."

- Exodus 34:6 (NIV)— And he passed in front of Moses, proclaiming, "The LORD, the LORD, the compassionate and gracious God, slow to anger, abounding in love and faithfulness..."

By reading and studying God's word you can personally see how faithful the Lord is toward those who trust and believe in him. This, in turn, will strengthen your own faith because according to Romans 10:17 "...faith comes from hearing, that is, hearing the Good News about Christ." Then you can begin to apply the word of God to your everyday life.

What does it mean to apply the word of God to your everyday life? How do we walk the word out? It means we have to acknowledge the war between our two natures, our flesh and spirit man, and decide that our spirit man will win. It means that we fight to kill our flesh daily. Through the power of the Holy Spirit we control our appetites for things of the world and desire more of the things of God. We apply it to our lives in our behavior, our practices and in our schedule. We change our conversation, where we hang out and with whom we hang with to please God. We treat God and our relationship with Him as though we are married to Him. We deny ourselves that we may fulfill FAITHFULNESS.

Faithfulness to what? Reading His word, your prayer life, and his instructions. Discerning and knowing His will and doing His will, letting go of your own plans, ideas and paths you may want, and think are best, to align with his plans and path for your life. Faithful to changing and becoming who you are called to be and not the person you think you are. In obedience, we submit to God and become as clay on the potter's wheel.

Jeremiah 18:1-4 (NLT) says, *"The Lord gave another message to Jeremiah. He said, "Go down to the potter's shop, and I will speak to you there." So I did as he told me and found the potter working at his wheel. But the jar he was making did not turn out as he had hoped, so he crushed it into a lump of clay again and started over."* Friend, it is time to produce the fruit of faithfulness. It's crushing time. Being crushed is uncomfortable yet necessary. Think of yourself as being on the wheel, being the jar that did not turn out as He, God had hoped. I know we think we don't need to change but we do. We need to be cleansed, delivered and made to be faithful. We do know how to be faithful because we've been faithful, but to all the wrong things. I know I'm right because we can be consistently rude, arrogant, quick tempered, selfish, greedy, bossy, grumpy, dishonest, boastful, immature, lazy, rebellious and some more. If I did not include the unclean spirit in you, you know exactly what it is. Whatever fruit of the flesh we are producing, God isn't pleased and it can't stay. We need to produce the fruit of the Holy Spirit. Galatians 5:22-23 (NLT), "But the Holy Spirit produces this kind of fruit in our lives: love, joy, peace, patience, kindness, goodness, faithfulness, gentleness, and self-control." John 3:6-8 (NKJV) says, "that which is born of the flesh is flesh, and that which is born of the Spirit is spirit."

Respond to God's faithfulness by being faithful and obedient. Spend quality time with Him. Give up some TV time or social media time to sit with Him to talk and listen. Start getting up an hour earlier for prayer before the business of your day begins. Commit to reading your word daily. Invite Him in every area of life. Connect with other praying women who are growing in Christ. I encourage you to complete this practical assignment, get an old-fashioned piece of paper and make a schedule from Sunday to Monday, block out time with God every day. Be faithful and honor God by keeping your appointment.

Faithfulness Compared to the Lemon

Lemons are a popular fruit that people use in small quantities to add flavor to food. However, they are rarely consumed alone due to their intense, sour taste. Alone, you can't mistake it to be anything else but what it is, a lemon.

Intense means done with great energy, enthusiasm, or effort. Intentional means what one intends to do or bring about. A determination to act in a certain way. Like the distinct taste of the lemon, our faithfulness and obedience to God should be intentional and intense because his faithfulness to us is just that, intentional and intense.

Lemons are used to add flavor to food. Lemons give flavor to baked goods, sauces, salad dressings, marinades, drinks, desserts, fish and meats. Drinking water with wedges of lemon in it has multiple health benefits. As you can see, there are many ways the lemon can be used and consumed. Likewise, we have many ways to display the fruit of faithfulness in every area of lives. May you please God and be blessed as you add the flavor of the fruit of the spirit, faithfulness to your life.

8

GENTLENESS

Presented by Desirée Fernandez

"To wit, that God was in Christ, reconciling the world unto himself, not imputing their trespasses unto them; and hath committed unto us the word of reconciliation."
2 Corinthians 5:19(KJV)

The dictionary defines gentleness as fairness, meekness, humility, moderation, gentle in condition. Another dictionary defines it as being kindly; amiable, not severe, rough, or violent; mild, moderate, or gradual.

The Avocado
The Avocado Reminds Me of the Fruit of Gentleness

An avocado is a large berry fruit, sometimes recognized as an alligator pear. It has dark-green, and almost black alligator-like skin, that may look unappealing externally. However, satisfaction is felt from its mild, not so sweet, buttery texture. The flesh of the avocado is a soothing light green. When pushing the avocado flesh from its skin, only a gentle push is required. The avocado is an under-utilized fruit that can be a good source of nutritional enjoyment. Just like the avocado, living with gentleness in a brutal world, just might sound unappealing. Nevertheless, we can delightfully partake of the satisfaction resulted from gentleness being involved in every layer and level of life.

Like the spiritual fruit of gentleness, an avocado is self-pollinating, without the aid of wind or insects. Gentleness is a characteristic that is not dependent on external responses that may not be first initiated. Changes are not (genetically) made in its character, and an avocado is able to maintain purity.

Comparisons between Gentleness and an Avocado

The Bible's definition of gentleness seems to require a little extra when it states mildness combined with tenderness. Like the extra for gentleness, there are additional reasons why an Avocado resembles the fruit of gentleness. A concern with self-pollination in an avocado, is that it can cause interbreeding and depression. Like the avocado, as we relate gentleness, we should also be aware of not internalizing an unbalanced lifestyle of gentleness to the extent of intimidation. When we apply Godly gentleness, we are able to reach out to others without internal weakness but drawing our strength from the vine-branch of the Holy Spirit from within whom we abide. We are then free to be gentle with people, without fear, or feeling vulnerable to their responses. Remember, gentleness is a verb. Although, gentleness may be subtle, it carries an anointing. The avocado may be a mild produce. However, it brings a burst of nutritional benefits. There moves power; in both gentleness, and the avocado.

Prayer of Strength with Gentleness

Our Father and our God, we pray through the name of Jesus. We pray in agreement, to ask you to give us this day, the seed of gentleness. Cultivate the circumstances of our lives to bear true fruit of gentleness that is rich in spiritual nutrients. Protect and deliver our fruit of gentleness at appointed times of benefit, to reflect right standing with you through the Spirit of Christ. Amen!

Declaration

We shall bring forth Christ-like fruit of gentleness to benefit the kingdom of God!

Gentleness that we witness from God

From the scope of observing our Creator, choosing at the beginning of time, to redeem the fall of man. Gentleness had to be at the forefront of God's love, when He implemented a plan of action that included Himself as atonement for our sin. He was not under obligation to bargain with creation. God could have chosen to start over completely, but instead He governed His plan over a period of generations. I believe that process displays gentleness. There is so much more we can know from God by observing HIS character through a wide scope, as well as through microscopic lenses.

Scripture(s)
- II Corinthians 10:1 "I am pleading with you, by the meekness and gentleness of Christ, who in the presence am slowly among you."

The Seed of Gentleness
- Ezekiel 17:5 (NKJV), "Then he took some of the seed of the land and planted it in a fertile field..."
- Ezekiel 17:8 (NKJV), "It was planted in good soil by many waters, to bring forth branches, bear fruit, and become a majestic vine."

We Are Called to Bear Good Fruit
Are you willing to yield to the seed of gentleness that the Holy Spirit has placed inside of you?

As the salt of the earth, our Christian representation should make a tremendous impact in maintaining world peace and preventing personal conflicts. In order for this to take place, the fruit of gentleness must be represented at round-table discussions as well as engaging at governmental affairs. Do not undermine the seed. Never underestimate the power of raising children to become future adults for the world they will someday be a part of. We are reminded of the scripture "Train up a child in the way he should go, and when he is old, he will not depart from it."

Scripture
- Philippians 4:5 says Let your gentleness be known to all men.

Prayer of Strength in Agreement for the Seed of Gentleness

Father God, from the moments we were converted to new birth in Christ, you have placed within us the Seed of Gentleness. Our dependency is in You, as our Provider and our Protector. We ask you, for the protection of our ear gates in defense of our fruit of gentleness. Deliver and guard our hearts and minds. We pray through the power of the Name of Jesus Christ. Amen!

Declaration
In defense of our harvest of fruit to come, we proclaim the protection of our seeds of gentleness for the Glory of God!

Process of the Development of Gentleness
Even with gentleness, Christians can carry the Presence of the Person of CHRIST. When GOD's people are submitted to HIS character, HE can use them, for HIS Glory. With true submission in CHRIST, GOD does not have a problem reaching lost people through yielded people. When JESUS preached, the people who

were the Called of GOD, heard HIM. By truth of HIS teaching, crowds of people followed and listened. The people were ready to hear and were drawn to the gentleness of GOD at actively at work.

The bible says, "My sheep know my voice, and they follow me. Revelation 2:29 (NKJV) says, "He who hath an ear, let him hear what the Spirit says to the churches." The Great Shepherd can gently draw people into Himself.

Personal Testimony

I had an employer, consistently and intentionally pursue infractions over a period of time. It wasn't just specific to me; it was a boastful office reputation. We witnessed colleagues respond in resignation, and others respond in retaliation. My previous experience with that, taught me to develop mature fruit, to address the subsequent matter ethically, professionally, and gently. Although it wasn't my own will, I humbled myself. I allowed The HOLY SPIRIT to speak from within and had to deepen my dependency on HIM daily. I wanted to keep my job and could not silence HIS inner voice. There were multiple days that I spent breaks feeding on scriptures. I could not exchange for the script of another voice, imposing toward my spiritual ear. Over time, we witnessed layers peel away. True change took place by the response of the employer. My public experience also helped a colleague witness the testimony and inquire about the difference. I was pleasantly surprised by their initiation and began to share strengthening scriptures. As a result, that colleague began to attend church, and experienced a turn around. In addition, one day, the employer asked me for prayer. Our work atmosphere began to shift. Only GOD can move in that way! Time given to maturity, has the benefits of developing the fruit of gentleness.

Scripture(s)
- Ephesians 5:2 With all lowliness and gentleness, with long suffering bear one another in a spirit of gentleness, considering yourself, unless you be tempted.
- 1Thessalonians 5:19 (Amplified) says, "Do not quench [subdue, or be unresponsive to the working and guidance of] the [Holy] Spirit.
- Jeremiah 17:8 For he shall be like a tree planted by the waters, which spreads out its roots by the river, And will not fear when the wind comes; But its leaf will be green, And will not be anxious in the year of the drought, Nor will cease from yielding fruit.

Comparison between the Developmental Process of an Avocado and Developing Gentleness

Through the process of The Holy Spirit developing gentleness in our character, we can respond to others, in representation of Christ, and give way for the Holy SPIRIT to take over a trespass even with a spirit of gentleness. Nevertheless, developing gentleness takes time yielded to sensitivities of God's assured Word. We must spend time abiding in the Holy Spirit and feeding on HIS WORD. When God is cultivating the fruit of gentleness in us individually, the process for application, reminds me of the necessary time needed to cultivate an avocado tree. Avocado trees are unique in the dedicated time needed for its tree to bear fruit. Avocado can remain good on the tree for months. Like the avocado, we need to prolong our time spent with GOD (abiding on the branch) through time given to relationship with GOD and drawing strength from GOD's Word as the fruit of gentleness is developed within us.

Prayer of Strength in Agreement for Developing the Character of Gentleness

Father God, you are our Provider and our Protector. We do not only want to call ourselves Christians in name. We want to rightly represent Christ, so that we do not take YOUR Name in vain. Strengthen our character of gentleness, to reveal the person of Christ. In Jesus Name we pray. Amen!

Declaration

For the development of our fruit, we proclaim to continue to abide in CHRIST, and to allow The WORD of GOD to abide in us for The Glory of GOD! We decree to grow and develop as the person of Christ!

Maturity of Gentleness

How do we navigate through unpreferable, commonly challenging, typical experiences with maturity in gentleness?

Our conduct displays the maturity in our fruit. Do we continue to abide on the vine, or are we prematurely given to external forces? Our point of connection on the tree is significantly important.

Personal Testimony

A couple of years ago, I experienced cardiac arrest. I didn't have previous cardiac issues and had just been discharged from the hospital the day before, for a severe headache. That morning I felt a tightening in my chest, that seem to cut off my breath. So, I began to walk toward the bedrooms to let my daughters know... However, before I could reach them, I apparently collapsed and went into cardiac arrest. My next awareness of consciousness was days later in ICU of the hospital. A breathing tube interfered with my ability to speak. I was aware of people coming in and out of the room. I attribute my healing to the prayers known and unknown, that went forth on my behalf. The timing of paramedic arrival was miraculous. The wisdom of the medical staff was priceless. The atmosphere through my time of healing was overwhelmingly bursting with peace. My body had experienced an event separate from my spirit. There was no room for fear or anxiety. I consider it to be GOD's overwhelming, gentle presence. I could feel strength and joy bursting from within. It really was awesome! The swift, but gentle actions of others were a tremendous blessing to me. My family visited and prayed. During my inability to speak for myself, my cousin also blessed me with a large prayer cloth, that she gently placed over my hospital bed. In silence, I could see the printed scriptures and proclaim them from within. Day and night, I meditated on GOD's healing WORD. The WORD was embedded in my sleeping thoughts as well. I felt comfort and assurance by GOD's evident Presence. The doctors were also astonished and pleased by my quick recovery. There is true power in the gentle presence of Almighty GOD Living in HIS WORD going forth!

Scripture(s)
- Jeremiah 17:8 For he shall be like a tree planted by the waters, which spreads out its roots by the river, And will not fear when the wind comes; But its leaf will be green, And will not be anxious in the year of the drought, Nor will cease from yielding fruit.

Comparison between the Maturing of an Avocado and the Maturing of Gentleness

In comparison, maturing of an avocado tree takes substantial cultivation and time! Maturity concerning gentleness is not generally instinctive and quickly reflective by nature. We are prepared over time, and time again, to mature in gentleness. In particular, avocado trees take a substantial amount of time to produce. Avocado trees can be costly to cultivate, but the need and demand, have made the avocados, some of the most valuable produce to grow. Like the avocado, gentleness may also be valued as having a costly anointing. GOD equips us with gentleness, that may serve as a lifeline to the needs of others. As the salt of the earth, our Christian representation that bears gentleness, has made a tremendous impact for maintaining peace.

Prayer of Strength for Becoming Mature in Extending Gentleness and Responding with Gentleness

Our FATHER and Creator, please help us to navigate through life's challenges and extend gentleness to all men, in right representation of CHRIST. Strengthen our relationships with you, that we may remain on the vine and reap the benefits of becoming mature in a Spirit of Gentleness. Through JESUS Name, we pray in Agreement. Amen!

Declaration
We decree that as a result of our yielding to God's work of gentleness in us, we are assured to reap a harvest of benefits!

Is It Good Fruit?

The Word says in Revelation 3:16, "God requires us to be fervently decisive." He wants us to walk firmly in maturity. Keep going forward in representation of Christ. We will bear the fruit planted by rivers of waters and bring forth fruit in due season if we walk up right before Him.

Matthew 12:33 (NKJ) says, "Either make the tree good and its fruit good, or else make the tree bad and its fruit bad; for a tree is known by its fruit."

I recall the story of a young man who had a drug addiction and planned to rob someone at gunpoint to get his next fix. He stood on the corner across the street and selected to approach a targeted man. However, upon his approach, the young man quickly discovered the gentleman was a pastor. The pastor began to minister to the young man in gentleness and shared his outreach ministry with the young man, who obliged. The dear minister soon became his pastor.

Scripture(s)
- Galatians 6:1 says, "Brethren if any man is overtaken in a trespass, restore such a one in a spirit of gentleness, considering yourself lest you also be tempted."

Comparison Between the Benefits of an Avocado and the Benefits of Gentleness

Just as GOD made the avocado's flesh is a soothing light green, to interest the eyes; possibly as a way of comforting us into eating what is good for us. Avocados are rich in nutritional value. The fruit of gentleness, likewise, has spiritual benefits that we can't do without. We need to feel the gentleness of GOD, in order to better appreciate the relationship that HE wants us to have with HIM. We need gentleness for our friends and family relationships. We must have gentleness to bring forth our babies into healthy maturity. We need gentleness for soft skills professionally. We also need gentleness when engaging strangers. We need gentleness to reach out to others in missions and ministering to the needs of others. Just as an avocado's nutrient benefits are plentiful externally for hair and skin, an avocado is just is internally beneficial for the heart. An avocado's substantial fatty content can be used for dipping or to spread in a multitude of dishes. It reminds me of the gentleness required for love, which covers a multitude of sins. The practice of applying gentleness in our everyday lives, holds much value and can deescalate unnecessary circumstances. The avocado's mild flavor allows a smooth enhancement to various healthful recipes. A mild manner of gentleness can also beneficially sensitize various life situations. Because the avocado has abundant nutritional factors for culinary recipes, it can discreetly be incorporated into interesting meals, as often as possible. We certainly need more gentleness in a competitive, self-seeking world. An avocado can be eaten as a raw fruit or used the main ingredient for a dish. It can be cooked, and it can be combined into soups. An avocado can also be sweetened, and delightfully complementary as a desert to top off a meal. Sometimes gentleness may be the main missing ingredient to turn a situation around.

Prayer of Strength in Agreement for Good Fruit

Fill us with YOUR gentle Presence Dear FATHER. Encourage our hearts and minds to give thanks in all things. Plant us each in advance, to bear good fruit and give testimony to the majestic power of your gentleness. We pray in Agreement, through The NAME of JESUS, The Anointed CHRIST. Amen!

Declaration
We declare the authority of CHRIST to rule in advance of life's situations for the Purposes of GOD with the fruit of temperance and gentleness.

Take-Aways

Throughout God's Word, HE has given us our first examples of gentleness. In continuance, we are gently being nurtured and replenished. Through the vine, God is investing in us, and developing us from within, giving overflow to our character.

When we abide in The Holy Spirit, God will give us power and grace to walk in gentleness with others. Maturity in gentleness, is a necessary process of sanctification. God matures us in the gentleness that we need in order to respond to others in the character representation of Christ. The maturity of our relationship with The Holy SPIRIT working through us, will be evident by our extension of sensitivities with others. This is the evidence of the fruit of gentleness that we are known by. The KJV of Matthew 7:20 is not only descriptive, it is also a mandate.

"Wherefore by their fruits ye shall know them."

My Disclaimer

I don't advocate anyone being swindled out of their earnings to pay for an "anointed" object of esteem. However, speaking from my personal testimony, it was beneficial to me as an intensive care patient, to have what is commonly called a prayer cloth conveniently within reach and sight. When the breathing tube interfered with my expression of voice, my visitors were able to read the printed scriptures over me. Although I could not speak for myself, I was truly able to read the powerful WORD of GOD, within my inner voice. Night and day, I proclaimed the healing scriptures over myself. In fervency of faith, activity was truly taking place. The HOLY SPIRIT provided true healing in gentleness. Having Scriptures to feed on, brings true action of change in our defense.

9

SELF-CONTROL

Presented by Andrea Taylor

"But the wisdom that is from above is first pure, then peaceable,
gentle, and easy to be intreated, full of mercy and good fruits,
without partiality, and without hypocrisy"
James 3:17 (KJV)

Self-Control, A Fruit Not Out of Season

Defining Self Control

The last characteristic listed in Galatians 5:22-23 as a fruit of the Spirit is self-control. Though it is listed last, there can be no doubt about its importance to living a Christian life. The fruit of the Spirit is the change in our character that comes about because of the Holy Spirit's work in us. We do not become a Christian on our own, and we cannot grow on our own. Philippians 2:13 (ESV) says that "it is God who is at work in you, both to will and to work for His good pleasure." Every good thing we do is the fruit of the Spirit's work in our lives.

Galatians 5:23 says self-control, which is temperance in the KJV bible, in Greek means "enkrateia" which means "possessing power", having mastered or possession of self-control. Temperance is moderation in thought, word or action. When we practice temperance, we are self-controlled and show restraint in behavior. The word also means "to get a hold of" or "to get a grip on". Self-control is the ability to control one's self, to use moderation, and the ability to say no to the desires of our flesh.

Self-control is thinking before acting and seriously considering the possible results.

A Nation Without Self Control

We live in a nation that has no self-control. Many of us have lives that are out of control and we don't even know it. Individual responsibility is dead and self-control is a foreign term even to those in the justice system of the United States, as we see week after week. We observe the current political scene daily as we view the evening news. We also see that people do what they want regardless of the impact to others in our society. According to the Wall Street Journal, most Americans feel our nation is out of control.

As people of God, we know that our nation is not really out of control in the sense that it is unrestrained, because God is still on the throne and has to allow it in order for anything to happen. It is out of control in the sense of each individual's own behavior because most people refuse to have self-control.

The Word of God in Isaiah 59:1-4, says "1Behold, the LORD's hand is not shortened, that it cannot save; nor His ear heavy, that it cannot hear. 2But your iniquities or lack of self-control have separated you from your God; and your sins your out-of-control behavior have hidden His face from you, so that He will not hear. 3For your hands are defiled with blood, and your fingers with iniquity; your lips have spoken lies, your tongue has muttered perversity. 4No one calls for justice, nor does any plead for truth. They trust in empty words and speak lies; they conceive evil and bring forth iniquity". (NKJV)

If that doesn't describe our nation at this point, there is very little that will. So really, sin is basically out of control behavior.

Anytime we give in to our raw lusts and desires, we have lost control of proper behavior and right thinking.

Many personal and societal problems stem from lack of self-control that greatly impact our, states, local cities and communities:

- Addictions– Only 10% of Americans dealing with addiction receive treatment
- Anger– America is dealing with 3 disasters, pandemic, economic and emotional calamities
- Divorce– 39% of marriages in America end in divorce
- Drug abuse– 19.7 million Americans battled substance abuse in 2017
- Greed– 50% of Americans have just 1% of the country's wealth
- Illicit sex– 25% of Americans have illicit sex outside their marriages
- Materialism– Many believe material possessions improve well being
- Murder– St. Louis, Missouri has the highest murder rate in America
- Rudeness– The City of New York and the State of New York are the rudest

Biblically, lack of self-control can be traced back to Genesis 4:2-12 (ESV) when Cain killed his brother Abel, or even further if we consider Satan's rebellion in Heaven, Ezekiel 28:12-15 (ESV). Cain refused to bring God his best and gave a mediocre sacrifice.

A lack of self-control is the natural tendency for human beings, as we see in the scriptures time and time again. I often think about the Israelites and their journey to the Promised Land. While Moses met with God on Mount Sinai, the Israelites quickly turned to idol worship and wild behavior. Exodus 32:25 indicates that Israel made herself a laughingstock to her enemies.

Understanding Our Old Nature

The main theme in Galatians is the struggle between our human sinful nature and the godly nature produced in us through the Holy Spirit. This struggle comes to a head with the final fruit of the Spirit, which is self- control. The question should be asked, who is in control of your life? The fallen state of humanity makes it impossible for us to control our sinful desires.

Only the Holy Spirit can develop self-control in us. Paul makes a distinction between freedom to sin and freedom to serve God. Freedom to sin is no freedom at all because it enslaves you to Satan, others and your own sinful desires.

Understanding What the Scripture Means by the Flesh

From a biblical perspective, the flesh is "that which is contrary to the spirit". Galatians 5:17 (NIV) the sinful nature wants to do evil, which is just the opposite of what the Spirit wants. And the Spirit gives us desires that are the opposite of what the sinful nature desires. These two forces are constantly fighting each other, so you are not free to carry out your good intentions.

The flesh and the Spirit are two opposing forces that exist within a believer. The Spirit is just that, the Holy Spirit. The flesh is the part of a believer that disagrees with the Spirit. The makeup of a believer is different from that of an unbeliever, in that an unbeliever does not have the Spirit of God indwelling them. In the case of an unbeliever, the flesh is in agreement with the Spirit of that unbeliever. Paul says in Roman 6:6 (ESV) " We know that our old self was crucified with him in order that the body of sin might be brought to nothing, so that we would no longer be enslaved to sin." What Paul is describing when he says "the body of sin" is the flesh.

The Greek philosopher Epictetus said, "No man is free who is not master of himself. None can be free who is slave to and ruled by his passions". We need to apply this to the weakest parts of our lives. It is almost impossible for us, in the flesh, to control ourselves. It is human nature to react in the manner in which others around us behave. The Bible teaches that for the believer to be in control of his life, he must allow the Holy Spirit to produce within him the characteristic of the Fruit of the Spirit, self-control. No person is master of himself if he allows the actions of others to dictate his behavior.

Living by the Spirit's Power

With regard to the use of the term controlled as in "controlled by the Spirit", the terms we use are often matters of semantics and our attempt to find words that express biblical concepts. Our terms need to be understood in the total context of the Scripture. For instance, Galatians 5:22-23 speaks of the fruit of the Spirit, i.e., that which is the product of the Spirit's work and ministry in the life of a believer. The fruit of the Spirit is the spontaneous work of the Holy Spirit in us, this is the result of our choosing to walk by the spirit. We must remember we are not puppets. It is a matter of accepting the fact of our own inability and weakness, but we do have the choice and responsibility to choose to walk by God's enablement or control, Galatians 5:16 (NLT) says "So I say, let the Holy Spirit guide your lives. Then you won't do what your sinful nature craves"

'Living by the Spirit's power' in Scripture denotes being governed by, ruled by, controlled by, or under submission to, and as believers we are to be governed by the Holy Spirit; ruled by

Him; controlled by Him and live-in submission to His leading and guiding in every part of our lives.

Regardless of how others may act toward us, we have the power because of the Holy Spirit to act and react in a godly manner. The Apostle Paul wrote in 1 Corinthians 6:12 (NLT) "You say, 'I am allowed to do anything'—but not everything is good for you. And even though "I am allowed to do anything," I must not become a slave to anything."

This passage means that certain things may be permissible, but they may not be profitable for our spiritual growth or the spiritual well-being of others. Our freedom in Christ, may be perfectly legitimate, but could deflect our attention away from Christ, or cause another believer to stumble, in which case we should avoid it, so as to keep ourselves from backsliding.

Self-Control Can Be Taught

a. Self-control is an important discipline that starts in our mind; we must set our minds to be disciplined. It is so easy to allow excuses to interfere in the discipline process. That disciplined mind will ignite a desire for more of Jesus, and then He will take up residence in our souls to satisfy us with His characteristics. To effect change in our character we need the Holy Spirit. Jesus said "If you hold to my teaching, you are really my disciples" John 8:31 (NLT). Discipleship includes learning the self-discipline of obedience.

b. Self-control is an important discipline that allows us to regulate our behavior. Jesus also said "if anyone desires to come after me, let him deny himself, and take up his cross daily, and follow me" Luke 9:23 (NKJV). Sin no longer has a hold on us, rather we have dominion and control over sin through the transference of power that Jesus provided on the cross.

Giving God Our Best

a. Church attendance

God's plan in this age involves the church, which Jesus promised to build (Matthew 16:18), and we should be supporting God's plan enthusiastically. "Let us consider how we may spur one another on toward love and good deeds, not giving up meeting together, as some are in the habit of doing, but encouraging one another, and all the more as you see the Day approaching" (Hebrews 10:24–25 NIV). The church is where our spiritual gifts best edify the body of Christ (Ephesians 4:11–12), and it is difficult to encourage each other to love and good works if we are not attending church. Christians should be committed, involved and supportive of their local church. This requires regular church attendance. A believer will naturally love his brothers and sisters in Christ (1 John 4:21 NIV), and that love will manifest itself in a desire to fellowship, not avoidance. When the church is praising the Lord, all believers should want to join in the praise; when the church is praying for others, all believers should want to join in the prayer; when the church is studying the Word, all believers should want to join in to learn.

b. Spiritual walk

A "walk" in the Bible is often a metaphor for practical daily living. The Christian life is a journey, and we are to walk it, we are to make consistent forward progress. The biblical norm for all believers is that they walk in the Spirit: "If we live in

70

the Spirit, let us also walk in the Spirit" (Galatians 5:25, KJV; cf. Romans 8:14). In other words, the Spirit gave us life in the new birth (John 3:6), and we must continue to live, day by day, in the Spirit.

To walk in the Spirit means that we yield to His control, we follow His lead, and we allow Him to exert His influence over us. To walk in the Spirit is the opposite of resisting Him or grieving Him (Ephesians 4:30 NIV).

c. **Strive for excellence**

God wants us to "become conformed to the image of His Son" (Romans 8:29 NIV). The Father wants all of His children to be like Jesus. He brings situations into our lives to refine us and chip away those flawed characteristics that are in the way of our becoming who He designed us to be (Hebrews 12:7; James 1:12 NIV). As Jesus was obedient to the Father in everything, so the goal of every child of God should be to obey our Heavenly Father (John 8:29). 1Peter 1:14–15 (NIV) says, "As obedient children, do not conform to the evil desires you had when you lived in ignorance. But just as He who called you is holy, so be holy in all you do."

When we surrender ourselves totally to Him, the Holy Spirit empowers us to love God fully and serve Him with the right motive. True service and holiness are simply the outworking of the Spirit, the overflowing of a life dedicated to the glory of God. When our focus is on *loving* God rather than simply *serving* Him, we end up doing both. If we skip the relationship, our service is of no use and benefits nothing.

d. **Give God the best moments of our days**

71

We cannot neglect spending time with God, both in private and corporately. We are absolutely called to invest time in relationships with others who don't know Christ and work hard in the things of life. We must remain focused on the things God has called us to do, working consistently to bring others to salvation.

More importantly, we need to schedule regular and daily time with God. It is He who equips us to carry out the tasks He has given us. It is He who directs our days. The worst thing we could do is manage our time as if it belongs to us. Time belongs to Him, so ask for His wisdom in how to best use it, then proceed in confidence, sensitive to His course corrections and be open to God-ordained interruptions along the way.

e. **Use our spiritual gifts to further the Kingdom**

One thing that is abundantly clear, God's command is God's enablement. If God commands us to do something (such as witness, love the unlovely, disciple the nations, etc.), He will enable us to do it. Some may not be as gifted at evangelism as others, but God commands all Christians to witness and disciple (Matthew 28:18-20; Acts 1:8). We are all called to evangelize whether or not we have the spiritual gift of evangelism. A determined Christian who strives to learn the Word and develop their teaching ability may become a better teacher than one who may have the spiritual gift of teaching, but who neglects the gift.

1 Corinthians 12:31 seems to indicate that this is possible: "but earnestly desire the best gifts." You can seek a spiritual gift from God and be zealous after it by seeking to develop that area. At the same time, if it is not God's will, you will not receive a certain spiritual gift no matter how strongly you seek

after it. God is infinitely wise, and He knows through which gifts you will be most productive for His kingdom.

No matter how much we have been gifted with one gift or another, we are all called upon to develop in a number of areas mentioned in the lists of spiritual gifts: to be hospitable, to show acts of mercy, to serve one another, to evangelize, etc. As we seek to serve God out of love for the purpose of building up others for His glory, He will bring glory to His name, grow His church, and reward us (1 Corinthians 3:5-8,14:1). God promises that as we make Him our delight, He will give us the desires of our heart (Psalm 37:4-5 NKJV). This would surely include preparing us to serve Him in a way that will bring us purpose and satisfaction.

The Supernatural Power of Self-Control

We spend our Christian lives waiting on something big to happen, completely oblivious to the fact that the greatest thing that could ever happen to us already did, and it's more than enough. A believer's life is designed to work with the Holy Spirit from beginning to end. The Holy Spirit encloses us in the loving will of God, seeding promise after promise in us, and sending power through us with His infallible word.

The Greek word Dunamis is used in the New Testament, to refer to inherent power, mighty strength and ability. 2 Timothy 1:7 (NKJV) says "For God hath not given us the spirit of fear; but of power, and of love, and of a sound mind."

The Holy Spirit enables us to gain control over our lives. The opposite of the spirit-controlled life is the life filled with the works of the flesh, and this is what Apostle Paul is saying in Galatians 5, those things that stand out as red flags in a life that's out of control.

One of the proofs of God working in our lives is the ability to control our own thoughts, words, and actions. It's not that we are naturally weak-willed, but that our fallen nature is under the influence of sin. Romans 6:6 (NLT) says, "We know that our old sinful selves were crucified with Christ so that sin might lose its power in our lives. We are no longer slaves to sin".

Without the power of the Holy Spirit, we are incapable of knowing and choosing how best to meet our needs. Even if we knew what would be best, such as not smoking, a sexual desire or some other need, would take precedence and enslave us again. As believers, we are caught in a cosmic struggle between our spiritual nature and our sinful nature. Believers need self-control because the outside world and internal forces still attack. Even the Apostle Paul was not able to remain in control of himself at all times. In the book of Romans 7:21-25 (NLT) Paul says "I have discovered this principle of life, that when I want to do what is right, I inevitably do what is wrong. I love God's law with all my heart, but there is another power within me that is at war with my mind. This power makes me a slave to the sin that is still within me. Oh, what a miserable person I am! Who will free me from this life that is dominated by sin and death? Thank God! The answer is in Jesus Christ our Lord. So, you see how it is: In my mind, I really want to obey God's law, but because of my sinful nature I am a slave to sin".

Self-Control is a Gift

Self-control is a gift that frees us. It frees us to enjoy the benefits of a healthy body. It frees us to rest in the security of good stewardship. It frees us from a guilty conscience. Self-control restricts the indulgence of our foolish desires, and we find the liberty to love and live as we were meant to.

    a.   Developed in us and through us by the Holy Spirit

b. We must acknowledge it comes from God, we are not the source

c. Take self-control by force by bringing ourselves under full control of the Holy Spirit

Lack of Self Control Weakens our Defenses

Like a vulnerable city, we must have defenses. A wall around an ancient city was designed to keep out the enemy. Judges at the gates determined who should be allowed in and who should remain outside. Soldiers and gates enforced those decisions. In our lives, these defenses might include avoiding close relationships with sinners, meeting with other believers, and meditating on the life-giving Word of God. We don't exhibit self-control if we continually deny that which would enslave us.

a. Admit there is a problem or a challenge; accept our past, acknowledging our short comings. James 1:14, Rom 14:12

b. Realize dysfunctional parents, home life or back grounds are not the cause

c. Acknowledge mistakes, past abuses and painful experiences were not the cause

d. Be completely honest with ourselves; admit that we enjoyed some of these behaviors

e. Identify our areas of weakness

f. Bring these weaknesses to God for total healing and deliverance.

How to Develop Self – Control

a. **Developing Self Control** - Genuine self-control or temperance involves the whole person, all of our faculties. Because we are created in the image of God, we are made after the pattern of God's trinity. The Godhead consists of God the Father, God the son and God the Holy Spirit; human beings consist of soul, body, and Spirit. The bible teaches us that Apostle Paul prayed that God would sanctify the Thessalonians wholly, completely, through and through and that their "whole spirit, soul, and body might be kept blameless" (1 Thess. 5:23 NIV). In this same manner, God's divine ideal is that we become self-disciplined in all three areas.

The Spirit is the part that permits awareness of God and communion with Him. The soul constitutes the very essence of our personality, that is comprised of intellect, emotions and will. The body, of course includes our physical being, and our senses and sensations. I think another way to express it is:

1. Our Spirit is God conscious
2. Our soul is self-conscience
3. Our body is world conscious

We can only be truly self-disciplined (controlled) if all three are engaged in this process. If you are a believer who ignores or neglects the spiritual side of your nature, you are incapable of experiencing self-control as it is presented in the bible. The concept itself is spiritual, therefore no carnal effort to achieve perfection can succeed.

The believer whose Spirit is dead in sin or not yielded to the Holy Spirit may at times achieve certain limited curbs and controls that may appear to be self-controlled, however, one entire dimension of personhood uninvolved (that is the Spirit dimension), genuine self-control is impossible.

For the unbeliever this means repentance, receiving Christ as Savior and being made spiritually alive. For the believer, it also means continuous commitment and cleansing and continuous filling by the Spirit, submitting to Jesus Christ. In Ephesians 5:18 Paul describes contrasting lifestyles as he admonishes us to "be not drunk with wine, wherein in excess: but keep on being filled with the Spirit". A person controlled by alcohol loses control and acts in an unrestrained and unbecoming manner.

A Spirit-filled person yields control to God and acts in a manner that is disciplined and becoming to God. To be filled with the Spirit is not to possess more of the spirit, for He indwells every believer in all of His fullness (Romans 8:9 and 1 Corinthians 6:19); rather, the Spirit possesses more of the believer, exercising full control over his or her faculties. When the Holy Spirit controls the human spirit, it, in turn, is able to control the soul (the seat of our personality and the part of us that is self-conscious) and body (that part of us that is world-conscious).

According to the remainder of Ephesians 5, evidence of the Spirit's control is praise, rejoicing, thanksgiving, and self-controlled submission in relationships. Jesus taught, "The spirit indeed is willing, but the flesh is weak" (Matthew 26:41) (KJV). Jesus is here referring to the human Spirit of the believer is providing the genuine, enduring motivation of self-control, because it has been brought into the control of the Holy Spirit.

b. **Know God's Word** –The first thing to enable us to cultivate self-control is knowing God's word. Scriptural memorization is also essential. God gives us the freedom to choose what we place in our mind. As believers, if we believe that the Bible is the written and infallible word of God, we must keep His word foremost in our mind. Memorization enables us to keep it constantly in the forefront of our minds, and that aids in helping us react to all life's circumstances according to God's precepts. One of my favorite scriptures is Joshua 1:8 (NLT) "Study this Book of Instruction continually. Meditate on it day and night so you will be sure to obey everything written in it. Only then will you prosper and succeed in all you do." Memorizing scripture also aids in our prayer life and meditation.

c. **Prayer** – When we think of Jesus who was without sin, who knew God's will completely, yet He was tempted. His response to those times of temptation was to pray and ask for strength to do what God wanted Him to do. He was God, but He was dealing with His human flesh. The bible talks about Jesus being tempted in the desert by Satan. There were three temptations concerning the flesh: turning stones into bread if you are the son of God; all kingdoms will be yours if you bow down and worship Satan; and throw yourself down from the pinnacle and let the angels catch you. These are the three temptations we have to overcome every day, those of the flesh, the devil, and the world. Jesus overcame these temptations through prayer and fasting.

The wonderful thing about prayer is that God meets us where we are. He comes alongside us to lead us into a deeper, more sincere relationship with Him, not motivated by guilt, but driven by His love. Prayer changes us, prayer changes lives, and prayer changes history. Our knowing God really makes us want to conform to Jesus and His will for our lives. God reveals Himself to us while we pray, and during these times we can more deeply understand and experience His love. One of the major outcomes of disciplined prayer is answered prayer.

Taken together, the spiritual disciplines of knowing God's word and consistent prayer life will lead and guide us into godly self-control.

What It Means to be Crucified with Christ

When we are saved by Christ's sacrifice, we are free (Galatians 5:1). That freedom includes, among other things, freedom from sin. "Our old self was crucified with him so that the body of sin might be done away with, that we should no longer be slaves to sin" (Romans 6:6). It means you've died to your old life and all its old desires, as the Spirit gives us self-control, we can refuse sin. Only as we freely admit that we cannot maintain a lasting self-control on our own will we be able to tap into God's self-control through the Holy Spirit. As in all the fruit of the Spirit, we ask him to replace our feeble efforts with his perfect control.

Being crucified with Christ means that we have a new love. The lusts of the flesh and the love of the things of this world have been crucified (Galatians 5:24). Now we love Christ, though we have not seen Him.

Christ died to set us free from a long list of laws and regulations, not free to do whatever we want because that would take us back to our own selfish desires.

Galatians 2:20 (NLT) is a key passage: "I have been crucified with Christ and I no longer live, but Christ lives in me. The life I now live in the body, I live by faith in the Son of God, who loved me and gave himself for me."

Being crucified with Christ is symbolic for a spiritual truth meaning that we are new creations. "This means that anyone who belongs to Christ has become a new person. The old life is gone; a new life has begun!" (2 Corinthians 5:17 NLT). The old life is dead and gone. We walk in newness of life.

The Supernatural Power of Christ

The purpose of God's supernatural power (resurrecting power) through His son Jesus Christ is to effect change in our character. His power not only gives us a new Spirit when we are born again, His power also produces a transformed life through the sanctification process (1 Peter 1:5 NLT).

God not only teaches us how to live through His Word, He also gives us the power to live through His Spirit. Ephesians 3:14–16 (KJV) says "For this cause I bow my knees unto the Father of our Lord Jesus Christ, of whom the whole family in heaven and earth is named, that He would grant you, according to the riches of His glory, to be strengthened with might by His Spirit in the inner man."

The Holy Spirit is the enabler, the executor, and the implementer of God's will becoming evident in our lives. Our responsibility is simply to make the choice to let Him do it. It's really a partnership. We offer our bodies as a "living sacrifice," God then is in us with His Spirit and accomplishes His will through us (Romans 12:1–2).

Christ is the perfect example of the manifestation of God's power. He lived His entire life depending upon this power. The Holy Spirit empowered Him to do all His miraculous acts and, of course, the Resurrection was the supreme manifestation of that power (Acts 2:24). The purpose of Christ's incarnation was to nullify the power of the devil and to free those held in bondage (Hebrews 2:14).

Jesus passed along this supernatural power to His disciples in order that they might accomplish the work He called them to do. "He called His twelve disciples together and gave them power and authority over all devils and to cure diseases... Behold, I give unto you power to tread on serpents and scorpions, and over all the power of the enemy: and nothing shall by any means hurt you" (Luke 9:1; 10:19 NKJV). The supernatural power the disciples received is, called "the resurrection power of Christ."

Christ then passed this same life-giving power on to us. This endowment took place at Pentecost when the Holy Spirit came upon thousands of believers and bestowed upon them a new and divine power (Acts 2:1–4 NKJV).

Developing self-control is only possible through the supernatural power of the Holy Spirit.

Steps to Sanctification

   a. **Focus on Our Model Jesus Christ –**
      We must work as the Holy Spirit works in us. We must work alongside God in the process of our sanctification. Paul says, "God works in us to will and do of his good pleasure." He gives us the very desires to grow in Christ and He works in us to do it. This is why when we get to heaven, there will be no room for boasting. Why?

Because God did it all. However, both realities are true. We must work and God is working.

1 Corinthians 15: 9-10 (NKJV) Paul says "For I am the least of the apostles and do not even deserve to be called an apostle, because I persecuted the church of God. But by the grace of God, I am what I am, and His grace to me was not without effect. No, I worked harder than all of them, yet not I, but the grace of God that was with me. "

In thinking of focus, I'm reminded of Peter trying to walk on water in Matthew 12. As long as his focus was fixed on Christ, he could walk on the water. However, when he started to focus on the wind and the waves, he began to sink. It is the same with us. We cannot grow in Christ if we are focused on anything other than him. Sometimes the trick of Satan is to get us focused on our sin, failures, or even the devil himself to stop our spiritual growth. However, the more we focus on our struggles the more we fail. Similarly, the more someone focuses on demons, conspiracy theories, or the world, the more they become consumed with them. This is the opposite of how to be sanctified. We are not to focus on sin or the world. We are to focus on Christ in order to be sanctified.

Paul said he wanted to know Christ. He wanted to know his power and have fellowship with his sufferings. For Paul, following Christ did not mean skipping the cross to go to glory, it meant being like Christ even in suffering. Paul said he pressed or ran after this since it was the reason that Christ took hold of him. Christ took hold of him for a relationship and for Paul to be made into Christ's very image. Therefore, Paul challenged the Philippians to pursue the same path he took—an endless pursuit of Christ as his goal (Phil 3:15-17). In order to be sanctified, like Paul, we must focus on Christ. He must be our ambition and focus.

b. **Know the Love of God**

Love is a tremendous motivation for spiritual growth. Paul said this: "For Christ's love compels us..." (2 Cor 5:14 NIV). Love motivated the great apostle to suffer, serve, and preach the gospel. The love of Christ compelled him. The love of Christ was constraining him to certain courses of action. He knew that Jesus out of His great love had given up His life for them. Jesus had willingly died for us all. In fact, Paul thought it was so important for the church to understand this love that he prayed for them to grasp it. Ephesians 3:17 (NIV) "And I pray that you, being rooted and established in love, may have power, together with all the saints, to grasp how wide and long and high and deep is the love of Christ, and to know this love that surpasses knowledge, that you may be filled to the measure of all the fullness of God."

He prayed for them to know Christ's love so that they may be "filled to the measure of all the fullness of God." To be "filled" means to be controlled and empowered by God, as noted in Ephesians 5:18. Similarly, if the Philippians could know how much God loved them, it would propel them in their spiritual growth, into working out their salvation.

I believe it is for this reason that Satan constantly works against believers knowing the love of God. In the beginning with Eve, Satan said, "Is it true that you cannot eat of every tree in the garden?" He wanted her to think God had deceived her, and that he was keeping the best from her. By doubting the love of God, she would be encouraged to sin. It was the same with Job. Satan, by bringing trials, was trying to get Job to curse God. Even his own wife said, "Why don't you just curse God and die?" Satan wanted Job to doubt the love of God because that would encourage him to sin and curse God. However, Job's reply to his trials was, "Even if God slay me, I will still trust him" (Job 13:5).

Many times, we must make ourselves vulnerable to get involved in other people's lives and their situations to really know the love of God. While serving others, God pours out His love in us to bless other people. Through these experiences we come to know God's love for us even more. I have experienced this when loving people who have hurt me. By forgiving and serving them, God gave me a supernatural love that I couldn't explain. When I look back at my life, during times of despair, and self-loathing, I realized I was looking for love in all the wrong places. Love is one of the greatest motivators in the world.

In order for us to be sanctified, we must know the love of God. For when we know the love of God, the depth, the height, and the width of it, will compel us to grow in our spiritually.

c. **Grow in Obedience to God**
Obedience to God is not only a necessary practice in sanctification but it is a proof of salvation. If believers who profess Christ do not practice daily obedience to God are deceived about their salvation. Jesus said this: "Not everyone who says to me, 'Lord, Lord,' will enter the

kingdom of heaven, but only he who does the will of my Father who is in heaven" (Matthew 7:21 NIV). Profession alone is not enough. Jesus said that in order to enter the kingdom of God one must be born again (John 3:3 NLT). A person that is born again has a new nature—a nature that desires to practice righteousness. Those who are truly part of the kingdom of God hunger and thirst for righteousness as Christ taught in the beatitudes as noted in Matt 5:6. 1 John 3:10 (NLT) says: "This is how we know who the children of God are and who the children of the devil are: Anyone who does not do what is right is not a child of God; nor is anyone who does not love his brother".

Those who obey God's word will be blessed by God. This doesn't necessarily mean wealth and health, though it doesn't necessarily exclude those things. It primarily refers to spiritual blessings. God reveals more to us through the word of God, more peace, and more fruit of the Holy Spirit.

Obedience to God's word protects us from stagnation and obstructing the sanctification process. Many of us are like the Israelites. We've listened to many sermons and preached word, seen the blessings, healings, and miracles of God but because our hearing isn't mixed with faith and obedience, we continue in the infancy stage without progression. We stay in the wilderness, a time of stagnation and remain undisciplined in our spiritual lives.

In order for the Israelites to leave the wilderness and go into the promised land, they had to practice obedience. This is a necessary component of our sanctification process too. Matthew 13:12 (NLT) "To those who listen to my teaching, more understanding will be given, and they will have an abundance of knowledge. But for those who are not listening, even what little understanding they have will be taken away from them."

This scripture means we are responsible to use what we have well. It's use it or lose it! When people reject Jesus, the hardness of their heart drives away and diminishes their comprehension of the word of God.

d. **Practice Continuous Discipline**
Philippians 2:12 (NIV) says "Therefore, my dear friends, as you have always obeyed, not only in my presence, but now much more in my absence, continue to work out your salvation with fear and trembling."

The phrase work-out is written as a command with a continuing emphasis. The idea is to keep on working out to completion, to ultimate fulfillment. This implies the need for continuous discipline in our spiritual lives. God gives us grace, but we must be disciplined in order to grow. We must "continually work it out" through the rest of our lives. We see this taught throughout the Scriptures. 1 Timothy 4:7, Paul told Timothy, "Discipline yourself unto godliness."

We must deny our nature and be willing to pursue Christ even when it isn't comfortable. Disciplining one's self for godliness requires a willingness to go outside of our comfort zone. We must continue to work out our soul salvation to completion.

e. **Develop Perseverance**
2 Peter 1:5-6 (NIV) says, "For this reason, make every effort to add to your faith goodness, and to goodness, knowledge and to knowledge, self-control, perseverance; and to perseverance, godliness." Self-control naturally leads to

perseverance as we value the long-term good instead of the instant gratification of the world. Again "work out" emphasizes to continually work out to completion and to ultimate fulfillment. In the NIV this is represented by the word "continue" to work out your salvation. This means that sanctification doesn't happen overnight. It is a process that must be worked out until it is fully completed which ultimately won't happen until we get to heaven. The implication of this is that we must persevere until it is complete. Perseverance in working out our salvation is important because of temptations we have toward becoming complacent, and apathetic believers.

In our journey of following Christ there will be temptations to give up the pursuit and just become spiritually comfortable and lethargic. The church is full of those who have not "persevered" in the discipline of "working out their salvation." In our churches today, there are so many mediocre believers unwilling to do anything for Christ. We see this with one church in particular in the New Testament, the church of Laodicea. In the book of Revelation 3:14 –17 (NIV) Jesus said to the church in Laodicea write:

> 14These are the words of the Amen, the faithful and true witness, the ruler of God's creation. 15 I know your deeds, that you are neither cold nor hot. I wish you were either one or the other! 16 So, because you are lukewarm—neither hot nor cold—I am about to spit you out of my mouth. 17 You say, 'I am rich; I have acquired wealth and do not need a thing.' But you do not realize that you are wretched, pitiful, poor, blind and naked".

The church in Laodicea had become lukewarm and thus distasteful and repugnant. The believers didn't stand for any, indifference and led them to idleness. By neglecting to do anything for Christ the church had become hardened, and self-satisfied and it was destroying itself. There is nothing more disgusting than half hardened in name only Christians who are self-sufficient.

This church was of no use to God, they were lukewarm. They thought to themselves that they did not need a thing. They were content and apathetic in their spiritual life, and therefore, they brought great displeasure to God. The church today is full of Christians who exhibit these behaviors. Practically, they are of no use, fit only to be disciplined by God. This is a temptation for all Christians. We must persevere in our work of being sanctified.

In Romans 12:11(NIV) Paul said this: "Never be lacking in zeal, but keep your spiritual fervor, serving the Lord". We all have this responsibility to persevere in our pursuit of holiness and fight against becoming apathetic, lukewarm believers.

We must fight against fatigue and being lethargic. Don't settle for following God halfway. Let Jesus Christ fire up your faith and get you into action.

> James 1:4 (NIV)says: "Let perseverance finish its work so that you may be mature and complete, not lacking anything".

f. Develop Healthy Fear

Healthy fear is reverential awe of God our Father. Proverbs 9:10 (NIV) says, the fear of God is the beginning of wisdom."

There is a fear, a reverential awe needed in the believer's life in order to continue to work out his salvation. This means we must see and know the awesomeness of God. When you truly realize how great and awesome God is, you will not give up intimacy and relationship with him for other things in this world.

Consider what David said about God, "Taste and see how good he is. See how awesome our God is." When you really know how wonderful He is, how can you choose the bitterness of sin over Him? When we really know how good He is, when we truly reverence God, it will be a motivation towards holiness. David sincerely referenced God and he wrote these words in Psalms 34:7-11:

> "7 The angel of the LORD encamps around those who fear him, and he delivers them. 8 Taste and see that the LORD is good; blessed is the one who takes refuge in him. 9 Fear the LORD, you his holy people, for those who fear him lack nothing. 10 The lions may grow weak and hungry, but those who seek the LORD lack no good thing. 11 Come, my children, listen to me; I will teach you the fear of the LORD."

David also says, there is protection and deliverance for those who revere God (7). Taste and see does not mean check out God's credentials, it's an invitation to try this, I know you'll like it. When we take the first step of obedience in following God, we discover He's so good and kind.

David says those who fear him will lack nothing, there are provisions for those who fear him (9). He speaks to those younger than him and says, "Listen, I will teach you the fear of the Lord" (11). The benefits are too good. You must revere God and make the reverence of the Lord your greatest pursuit.

If we are going to be sanctified, we must reverence God, fear his discipline, and revere his word. Believers should minister with a holy fear and trembling of the one they serve. Consider how Paul described his ministry to the Corinthian church: "I came to you in weakness and fear, and with much trembling" (1 Corinthians 2:3 NIV). Paul was a man who lived in reverential fear of God. We know Paul had a reverential fear by his words, his faith and how he served God. He served with a constant view of a majestic God, a God who is a "consuming fire" (Hebrews 12:29 NIV).

g. **Allow God to Work in us**
   1. **God works in us to give us his desires**
   In John 16:8, (NIV) Jesus said when the Holy Spirit comes, "he will convict the world of guilt in regard to sin and righteousness and judgment". Even though Christ was speaking to the world, this certainly happens to believers as the Spirit produces in them a desire to do God's will.

   2. **God works in us to convict us of sin.**
   I've read this is called a holy discontent. By the Holy Spirit's convicting work in our heart, he enables us to hate and despise our sin. He does this through God's word, fellowship with believers, and through discipline. Consider how Isaiah responded when he saw God: "'Woe to me!' I cried. 'I am ruined! For I am a man of unclean lips, and I live among a people of unclean lips, and my eyes have seen the King, the LORD Almighty'" (Isaiah 6:5 NIV). By seeing God, it revealed to Isaiah how sinful he and his people were.

Similarly, Paul said this: "O wretched man that I am" (Romans 7:24) (NKJV). The Holy Spirit convicts us of sin, enabling us to hate it and to desire to get rid of it. He gives us a holy discontent.

3. **God gives us holy aspirations.**

God gives us holy aspirations, desires to be more like Him or to fulfill His will. We see both Paul's holy discontent and his holy aspirations in Philippians 3:12-14, (NIV) "[12] Not that I have already obtained all this, or have already been made perfect, but I press on to take hold of that for which Christ Jesus took hold of me. [13] Brothers and sisters, I do not consider myself yet to have taken hold of it. But one thing I do: Forgetting what is behind and straining toward what is ahead, [14] I press on toward the goal to win the prize for which God has called me heavenward in Christ Jesus. Paul desired to press on to be more like Christ daily, he had holy aspirations.

4. **God works in us by convicting us of judgment.**

The Holy Spirit reminds us of the coming judgment and the second coming of Christ. As believers we will not be condemned for our sins, but we will be rewarded or lose rewards based on our works. 2 Corinthians 5:9-11 (NIV) says:

> "So, as believers we must make it our goal to please him, whether we are at home in the body or away from it. For we must all appear before the judgment seat of Christ, that each one may receive what is due him for the things done while in the body,

whether good or bad. Since, then, we know
what it is to fear the Lord, we try to
persuade men. Paul said that he and the
other apostles were motivated by the
judgment seat of Christ."

When we are absent from our bodies, we can't do
anything about pleasing God. I'm so thankful that
day has not come! So, we as believers must consider
there are many opportunities while we are present
in our bodies to please God.

When we get to heaven there will be no more need
for faith, no more need for endurance through trials,
no more need for courage and boldness in telling
others about Jesus. Now, while we are present in
these bodies, it is our only opportunity to please God
in these areas of our lives.

> [15] "If any man's work shall be burned, he
> shall suffer loss: but he himself shall be
> saved; yet so as by fire."

1 Corinthians 3:15 talks about those who will be
saved by fire (KJV), meaning they will receive no
reward in heaven. The Holy Spirit convicts us of this
judgment.

5. God works in us by giving us the power to work.

Philippians 2:13 says, "For it is God who works in
you to will and to act in order to fulfill his good
purpose (NIV)."

The Greek word for "act" in verse 13 is "energio". Our English word energy is derived from "energio". God energizes and empowers us to do His will. In Colossians 1:28-29 (NIV) "We proclaim him, admonishing and teaching everyone with all wisdom, so that we may present everyone perfect in Christ. To this end I labor, struggling with all his energy which so powerfully works in me". The Apostle Paul said he labored to exhaustion and the reason he could do that is because the power of God worked in him so strongly.

My Filthy Habit

Addiction is a term that means compulsive physiological need for and use of a habit-forming substance (cocaine, heroin or nicotine), characterized by tolerance and well-defined physiological symptoms upon withdrawal. It has also been used more broadly to refer to compulsive use of a substance known by the user to be physically, psychologically, or socially harmful.

In Titus 1:7 and 2:3, 1 Timothy 3:3 and 3:8, (NIV) the bible says those who are addicted or given too much wine, drunkards or heavy drinkers are disqualified from teaching or holding a position of authority in the church.

It's clear that church leadership needs to be sober and self - controlled so that, by their example, they can teach others to be the same. For we know that the word teaches us in 1 Corinthians 6:10 that "drunkards" shall not inherit the kingdom of God. As believers, we must not be dependent upon alcohol, and it stands to reason neither, tobacco, drugs, pornography, nor gambling. Read 1 Corinthians 6: 9-10 (NLT):

[9] Don't you realize that those who do wrong will not inherit the Kingdom of God? Don't fool yourselves. Those who indulge in sexual sin, or who worship idols, or commit adultery, or are male prostitutes, or practice homosexuality, [10] or are thieves, or greedy people, or drunkards, or are abusive, or cheat people, none of these will inherit the Kingdom of God."

After going through a very difficult time in my life I began to smoke cigarettes. In the beginning it was something I did socially with friends who smoked too. I was a very young woman at that time and I told myself I could quit whenever I decided to. However, that wasn't true. More than anything I wanted to be delivered from this addiction. Smoking cigarettes affects the respiratory system, the circulatory system, the reproductive system, the skin, and the eyes, and tobacco increases your risk to develop so many different cancers.

Cigarettes generate secondhand smoke which is smoke that has been exhaled, or breathed out, by the person smoking. Tobacco smoke contains more than 7,000 chemicals, including hundreds that are toxic and about 70 that can cause cancer.

In addition to second, it also produces third-hand smoke that is the lingering smoke smell that can be found on anyone or anything after it has been exposed to the aftermath of a cigarette. It's tobacco smoke contamination that remains after the cigarette has been extinguished. Like I said, it's a disgusting habit!

According to the World Health Organization (WHO) there are 1.3 billion smokers in the world today. Tobacco kills more than eight million people a year, translating to one smoking related death every five seconds. People and acquaintances, I knew during that time in my life were suffering from the effects of smoking.

Although the bible does not directly mention smoking, the principles of self-control apply. The bible commands us not to allow our bodies to be mastered by anything. "Everything is permissible" according to 1 Corinthians 6:12, (NLT) "we are allowed to do anything, but not everything is good for us".

Because my desire to quit smoking was so poignant, I sought God's help through prayer. Because I wanted guaranteed success, I applied the following steps to my deliverance:

1. I took authority over my addiction to cigarettes in my mind and Spirit first. I declared that I was a righteous woman and that God had saved me and filled me with the Holy Ghost.

2. Through prayer and supplication, I asked God to deliver me from this disgusting habit; 1 Corinthians 6:19-20 (NLT) says:
   "Don't you realize that your body is the temple of the Holy Spirit, who lives in you and was given to you by God? You do not belong to yourself, for God bought you with a high price. So, you must honor God with your body".

3. I believed God's word in Ephesians 3:20, (KJV) "Now unto him that is able to do exceedingly abundantly above all that we ask or think, according to the power that worketh in us". So now, caring for my health was not just a matter of good stewardship, it was a matter of reverential piety.

4. Realizing it may take more than one attempt to quit and get it right, I focused on Titus 2:12 (NIV) "It teaches us to say no to ungodliness and worldly passions, and to live self-controlled, upright and godly lives in this present age." In my mind, I strategized how I would achieve success and be delivered from this addiction. Some days were harder than others. As a fallible human being I was prone to delusion and had to remind myself of the tricks of the enemy; the importance of remaining sober-minded, alert, and vigilant against the wiles of the devil. 1 Peter 5:8 (NIV) "Be sober-minded; be watchful. Your adversary the devil prowls around like a roaring lion, seeking someone to devour."

5. During this time in my life and career, I socialized with many people who were not believers. Their lifestyles didn't always align with how I lived, so I limited my interaction with them. Assuring that I would not encounter and interact with any smokers once I decided that I would be delivered.

6. I purposely did not interact with anyone who did not have a relationship with God. Going forward, I terminated relationships with acquaintances and professional colleagues who smoked and drank socially.

7. Often times, being in the presence of people who are not like minded, will prohibit the success of your total deliverance. Every effort I made was a step toward my goal, and it was an essential part of this journey.

8. I ascertained the best time to accomplish this goal. I planned my deliverance over the Great American Cancer Society Smoke Out Weekend.

9. Thanks be to God for His holistic approach to deliverance. My God delivered me from cigarettes and nicotine. Hallelujah!

My Most Difficult Trial: Marijuana

My struggle with marijuana addiction developed later in life, and I grappled with this issue for years. Making the decision to change and deciding what that change would look like was an arduous process and did not occur over night. It was something I knew I had to do, so I contemplated, and prayed about it, knowing that I could not do this on my own. I needed God's help to accomplish this goal. Many times, I considered getting professional help. I was so ashamed and embarrassed! One thing I knew, was that I wanted total and complete deliverance from this albatross around my neck. Only with the help of God!

My preparations included removing and distancing myself from people who had been a part of my life and inner circle for years. Many of these friends were single mothers like myself, struggling to provide a decent home for our children and oftentimes working long hours to pay our mortgages. This circle included many family members, who consistently arrived on my doorsteps with joints, and marijuana from countries that they wanted me to sample. During this preparation and as I made my elimination list, I realized there were so many friends and family on this list, practically my entire inner circle. However, my mind was made up; I desired a changed life.

Quitting addictive behavior is very difficult. Extinguishing social relationships that are intertwined with the behavior are necessary. I was unable to establish a support network because the people I knew professionally and spiritually didn't know I had

97

this problem. My shame and embarrassment overwhelmed me, I was fearful and emotionally wrought! I had no one I could talk to but God. So, I prayed, and asked Him for wisdom toward deliverance.

Many addictions mask underlying emotional issues, unresolved issues that may stem from childhood experiences. Often times, these traumatic experiences have not been dealt with nor resolved. Unresolved family issues in dysfunctional families can surface in the form of addiction. Numerous situations from our immediate families have plagued us our entire lives.

Let me be clear, going through this was one of the most painful, difficult and frustrating struggles of my life. There were many failed attempts before I succeeded; I never stopped trusting God, I knew He would deliver me, if I just held out. God is so faithful.

The fruit of self-control enabled me to succeed and overcome my addiction. In the King James Bible translation, the word temperance is used and often translated as self-control, but perhaps the meaning of this word would be communicated more accurately if it were defined as passion-control. A person with temperance has been enabled by the Holy Spirit to bring their passions under control and the subjection of their renewed mind, rather than to allow their passions to control their will.

The word self-control gives the wrong impression here because it is not self that gives this control. The Greek word εγκρατεια is a fruit of the Spirit, which means the Spirit is the one who does the controlling. Many believers who struggle with addiction soon realize that self cannot provide this control. Thus, a focus on self-control is futile. What we need instead is Spirit-control, which is the very point of the passage in Galatians 5 (KJV). A Spirit-given self-control is inherently contradictory. Temperance is an accurate translation because the word does not focus on self.

Temperance as a character trait is a common theme throughout the KJV Bible, especially in the New Testament. Temperance or self-control is one of the fruit the Holy Spirit produces when He indwells believers (Galatians 5:22). It is impossible to live a godly life and please the Lord without temperance (self-control) because our flesh wants only to please itself (Romans 7:21–25). Romans 13:14 (KJV) warns us to "make no provision for the flesh and its lusts." However, some people mistakenly believe that temperance means we can dabble in sin as long as we are not overcome by it. That's not what this verse says. It implies that along with temperance we exercise caution and wisdom. When we desire to please the Lord, we will stay far away from anything that has the appearance of evil. We cannot live temperance lives and commit sin, even though we might believe we can control our behavior. The world has been telling us for years that marijuana is not an addictive substance. So many have been deceived by this belief.

Paul describes biblical temperance in 1 Corinthians 9:27 (NKJV): "But I discipline my body and bring it into subjection, lest, when I have preached to others, I myself should be disqualified." Even Paul knew the power of the flesh could topple his ministry, so he refused his flesh what it craved in order to develop strength of character. Today's news headlines often remind us of the foolishness of attempting ministry without temperance. When a Christian leader falls, it is almost always due to a lack of temperance and lack of personal discipline.

Even though it's difficult, and a complete withdrawal from addictive substance may take some time, we can look to God for whom our help comes from. We set our hearts on things above and pray God will give us strength to have victory in this trial. God has declared that His grace is sufficient (2 Corinthians 12:9) (NKJV). Where we are weak, He is strong. The desire for these substances will be reduced as we grow and gain strength in God. The power of God will alleviate the pressure to use addictive substances, all to His glory! "I can do all things through Christ who strengthens me" Philippians 4:13 (NKJV).

I praise God for His deliverance from addictive substances in my life!

Believe What God Say's About You

a. **You are fearfully and Wonderfully Made**

> **Psalms 139: 14 (KJV)** - Thank you for making me so wonderfully complex! Your workmanship is marvelous, how well I know it.

> The human body is the most complex and unique organism in the world, and that complexity and uniqueness speaks volumes about the mind of its Creator. Every aspect of the body, down to the tiniest microscopic cell, reveals that it is fearfully and wonderfully made. The human brain is also an amazing organ, with the ability to learn, reason, and control so many automatic functions of the body. Our brains can control our heart rate, blood pressure, breathing, and to maintain balance to walk, run, stand, and sit, all while concentrating on something else.

> We are made in God's image. Having the "image" or "likeness" of God means, in the simplest terms, that

we were made to resemble God, not in the sense of flesh in blood, but in the Spirit. Scripture says that "God is spirit" (John 4:24) (KJV) and therefore exists without a body. "For God is Spirit, so those who worship him must worship in spirit and in truth."

b. **You Have Been Chosen**
Ephesians 1:4 (KJV) - Even before he made the world, God loved us and chose us in Christ to be holy and without fault in his eyes. We belong to Him through Jesus Christ. He looks at it as if we had never sinned.

c. **You Are a New Creature in Christ – 2 Corinthians 5:17 (KJV)**
This means that anyone who belongs to Christ has become a new person. The old life is gone; a new life has begun! The Holy Spirit gives us new life. Anyone who is in Christ is a new creature.

d. **Your Body Is the Temple of the Holy Spirit – 1 Corinthians 6:19 (KJV)**
Your body is the temple of the Holy Spirit, who lives in you and was given to you by God. You do not belong to yourself; you no longer own your body.

e. **You Have Been Called to be a Saint- 1 Corinthians 1:2 (KJV)**
To the church of God that is in Corinth, to those who are sanctified in Christ Jesus, and called to be saints, with all those in every place who call on the name of our Lord Jesus Christ, their Lord and ours.

This call is applicable to all believers.

f. **In Christ Jesus You Have Wisdom,
    Righteousness, Sanctification and Redemption
    – 1 Corinthians 1:30 (KJV)**
    "But of him are ye in Christ Jesus, who of God is
    made unto us wisdom, and righteousness, and
    sanctification, and redemption:"
    God is the reason we have a relationship with
    Jesus Christ, who became for us wisdom from God,
    righteousness, sanctification, and redemption. Our
    union with God results in us developing His
    attributes.

g. **Redeemed – Colossians 1:14 (KJV)**
    "In whom we have redemption through his blood,
    even the forgiveness of sins."

    Redemption means repurchased. We have bought for
    a price, which is the blood of Jesus Christ. God
    allowed Jesus His son, to die on the cross. In effect,
    we are so valuable that we are worth Jesus to our
    Father, God.

h. **Accepted - Romans 15: 7 (NLT)**
    "Therefore, accept each other just as Christ has
    accepted you so that God will be given glory."

    One of our greatest needs as human beings is to be
    accepted, and our Lord and Savior has accepted us
    forever. This acceptance is based upon what He has
    done not what we have done. This is an acceptance
    of our deepest Spirit that will be set free from sin
    and death. He does not accept our sin, but accepts us

in spite of our sin. Our hearts long to please Him because of what He has done.

i. **Forgiven – Colossians 2: 13-14 (KJV)**
We had a debt that we could not pay, but Christ paid our debt on the cross. His death resulted in all our transgressions to be forgiven, even future transgressions. Now, when we seek forgiveness, we are appropriating the forgiveness that is already ours.

j. **Justified – Romans 5:1 (KJV)**
Justification is the act of God not only forgiving the believer's sins but imputing to him the righteousness of Christ. The Bible states in several places that justification only comes through faith. Justification is not earned through our own works; rather, we are covered by the righteousness of Jesus Christ. The Christian, being declared righteous, is thus freed from the guilt of sin. God disciplines us in order to help us experience the abundant life He has planned for us. (John 10:10)

k. **Reconciled – 2 Corinthians 5:18 (KJV)**
Our sin alienated us from God, but because of Jesus our mediator, made the sacrifice for us, He made our relationship with God perfect. We've been reconciled back to God.

l. **Made Perfect – Hebrews 10:14 (KJV)**
When Jesus died in our place and paid our debt, all our imperfections were forgiven in the eyes of God. He declares us perfect by Jesus Christ's death on the cross.

m. **Righteous - Philippians 3:9 (KJV)**
In heaven an exchange was made, all of our unrighteousness was placed on Jesus Christ and His righteousness was placed on us. This is known as the imputed righteousness of God. So, now when God looks at us, He sees the righteousness of Christ.

n. **Given Access – Ephesians 2:18 (KJV)**
For through Him we both have access by one Spirit unto the Father.

Jesus has brought us before the Father and we have access to the Father throughout eternity. We have access and will never be excluded. This is why we must always trust that the Father hears our petitions for Him to direct our steps.

Fruit: What a Christian Life is All About

My natural fruit is pineapple. It's the perfect fruit to eat on a hot summer day and it's naturally the queen of all fruits because it has a crown. Pineapples are also considered an expression of welcome throughout the south and symbolizes the values we appreciate in our home, friendships, hospitality and warmth.

A Christian life is about bearing fruit. God's expectation for us as believers is to walk in Spirit and to bring forth fruit. In John 15:16 (NKJV) Jesus said "You did not choose me, but I chose you and appointed you that you should go and bear fruit, and that your fruit should remain, that whatever you ask the Father in My name He may give you".

What is the Pineapple?

The definition of a pineapple is a tropical fruit (or plant) with a tough outer shell that looks like a pine cone with edible yellow fruit inside. The ovoid fruit of the pineapple plant, which has very sweet yellow flesh, a tough, spiky shell and a tough, fibrous core. Botanically, the pineapple is known as a multiple fruit (or plant) or a collective fruit which is formed from a cluster of flowers called an inflorescence. An inflorescence is a group or cluster of flowers arranged on a stem that is composed of a main branch or a complicated arrangement of branches. The fruit is a seed-bearing structure that develops from the ovary of a flowering plant, however, because of the complicated structure of the pineapple it is also known as a plant consisting of roots, leaves and stems.

Unlike most fruits, pineapples are not grown from seeds. On occasion, pineapples produce tiny black seeds just below the peel of the fruit, which can be seen if you're peeling the fruit, but generally, pineapples are highly self-incompatible. Self-incompatibility is a mechanism that prevents pollen from one flower from fertilizing other flowers of the same plant. Despite this self-incompatibility, the plant will still develop because pineapples are parthenocarpic[3] which means the plant (fruit) develops without fertilization of the ovary. Most fruits require fertilization for fruit development. Another example of a parthenocarpic fruit is a banana.

History of the Pineapple

---

[3] Parthenocarpy refers to the development of fruit without fertilization. The process produces a sterile fruit that lacks seeds.

The pineapple originated in South America, where it has been cultivated for many centuries. The introduction of the pineapple to Europe in the early 1600, made it a significant cultural icon of luxury. This fruit is neither a pine nor an apple, but a fruit consisting of many berries that have grown together. The origins of those terms stem from the same time period when the European explorers of the Americas brought the fruit to Europe, using the word pineapple due to its resemblance to a pinecone from conifer trees. Christopher Columbus brought the plant back to Spain and called it piña de Indes, meaning "pine of the Indians."

During this time, pineapples were so rare that only the richest of people would eat them. Sometimes they would not even eat the fruit, instead they would have viewing parties and display the pineapple until it rotted completely. Later pineapples became a sign of hospitality in the new world. If a hostess was able to get her hands on a juicy pineapple, she would be the talk of the town. People were excited to attend such a party because they knew that the hostess had spared no expense for them.

Since the 1820s, the pineapple has been commercially grown in greenhouses and many tropical plantations. It is the third most important tropical fruit in world production. In the 20th century, Hawaii was a dominant producer of pineapples, especially for the US; however, by 2016, Costa Rica, Brazil, and the Philippines accounted for nearly one-third of the world's production of pineapples.

How the Pineapple is Grown

I've always thought of the pineapple as a fruit, however it's not. In fact, it is a part of the stem of the plant and it becomes bulbous in the middle and then has leaves sprouting from the top. It rises from the center, and then it has spiked leaves on it. So, it is actually a branch of the tree or a branch of a plant and not a fruit. The pineapple plant does not reproduce from seeds, but instead new plants form from the roots of the main plant or from the crown of the fruit.

The plant is actually the result of dozens of individual fruit-producing flowers or berries that have fused into a single fruit. When flowering, it appears as a cluster of blossoms on a single stalk; bulbous pink and green blossoms grow in the crown of leaves. The technical term for this is a "multiple fruit" or a "collective fruit." Multiple fruits, or collective fruits, are fruiting bodies formed from a cluster of fruiting flowers. The pineapple is a fruit (plant) that carries its roots along with it.

The pineapple grows out of the top of the central stem of the plant and is the most valuable material in growing the plant. When removed, the crown of the pineapple plant contains small roots. The little brown spots which most people think are thorns are actually the roots of the plant.

If it's planted into the ground (or a pot), a new fruit-producing plant will grow. The pineapple plant only flowers at full maturity, which may take up to two-three years and only produces one pineapple. Then it dies. But before it dies it also produces offspring. Suckers or pups are little plantlets that grow between the leaves of the mature pineapple.

Medicinal Value

I simply love pineapples because not only do they taste good, they're very good for you. Eating fresh pineapple lifts and enhances my mood, giving me a much-needed energy boost. Pineapples are full of bromelain which is very good for you; it's an anti-inflammatory, muscle relaxant, and digestive aid.

Bromelain is a protein-digesting enzyme mixture derived from the stem, fruit, and juice of the pineapple plant. It has a centuries-long history of being used to treat medical ailments, primarily throughout Central and South America. Bromelain is also used as a digestive aid, for osteoarthritis, and to reduce soreness in aching muscles. The pineapple is the only unique kind of bromeliad produced in an edible plant. It's perfect to eat on a hot summer day, and naturally the queen of all fruit because it has a crown! Listed are a few other medicinal values:

- Pineapples are especially rich in vitamin C, which is essential for growth and development, a healthy immune system and aiding in the absorption of iron from the diet.

- Manganese, a mineral that's important for developing strong bones and connective tissue is another health benefit in pineapple. Manganese aids growth, maintaining a healthy metabolism and contains antioxidant properties.

- Pineapples also contain trace amounts of vitamin A and K, phosphorus, zinc and calcium.

- Studies have shown that pineapple and its compounds may reduce the risk of cancer because they may minimize oxidative stress and reduce inflammation.

- Pineapple is rich in other minerals such as potassium and copper. Potassium can help increase blood flow throughout the body by relaxing your blood vessels to allow circulation in a less restricted manner.

- Eating pineapple can help reduce blood clots and the risk of atherosclerosis[4], stroke, and heart attack; copper aids in red blood cell formation, which can increase cognitive abilities and ensure your organs function at optimal levels, which can lower the chance of neural disorders such as dementia or Alzheimer's.

A Pineapple Perspective in Maturity

In my examination of the pineapple and its growth cycle, I thought this plant's growth and development mirrors the transition believers undergo when they are growing and developing in Christ.

Based upon the information shared, I have changed my perspective on the pineapple. The pineapple has not changed, but my thoughts on the pineapple have changed; what I know about the pineapple has changed. We must develop a new thought process as we broaden our mind and understanding of spiritual disciplines. The length of time it takes for a pineapple to mature reminded me of the time needed to develop spiritual maturity and disciplines to become true followers of Christ.

It can take three years for a single pineapple to mature. That is a very long time for a plant (or fruit) to grow to maturity. In colder climates it may take even longer. Once a pineapple flowers you have to wait for another six months for the fruit to mature. This information was truly amazing and difficult for me to conceive; however, I suppose the length of time to mature for the pineapple (reference tropicalpermaculture.com) is significantly

---

[4] Atherosclerosis - A buildup of cholesterol plaque in the walls of arteries causing obstruction of blood flow.

shorter than the time needed for some believers to develop into mature Christians.

It takes a significant amount of time for many of us to flourish into that "ananas comosus" (another name for mature pineapple). As with knowledge of the pineapple, Christian maturity requires a change in our perspective viewpoints on life and how we apply God's word. It requires a radical reordering of our priorities, changing over from pleasing self to pleasing God and learning to obey God. The key to maturity is consistency, perseverance in doing those things we know will bring us closer to God. We must change our perspective on how we think about everyday living, how we interact with our loved ones and those who enter into our sphere of life. It is learning to walk under the instruction of another, the Holy Spirit. Being filled with the Spirit means we walk under the Spirit's control. As we submit more and more to the Spirit's control, we will also see an increase in the fruit of the Spirit in our lives.

When contrasting the length of time, it takes for the pineapple to reach its maturity to the Christian walk, three years seems insignificant. Depending upon a believer's outlook, it could take many more years before reaching maturity. Many believers never accomplish this goal. We are all works in progress. Being effective and fruitful, in the knowledge of our God, is the essence of spiritual maturity.

The Pineapple Principle

Oftentimes, I'm faced with challenging tasks and projects that can sometimes be overwhelming. I believe God is teaching me to slow down and learn how to use my time wisely. Underestimating the amount of time needed to complete tasks and projects to my satisfaction is a flaw, which causes me frustration and anxiety.

110

God is guiding me to take my time and to enjoy the task from beginning to completion. He is showing me how to spend more time planning my approach prior to orchestrating the task. In order to complete the work, He has assigned us, it is essential we make the best possible use of our time daily. Time is a gift from God and none of us knows how much time we are allotted.

Ephesians 5:15–16 (KJV) says, "See then that ye walk circumspectly, not as fools, but as wise, redeeming the time, because the days are evil." When God says we should be redeeming the time, He wants us to live in constant awareness of that ticking clock and make the most of the time we have. The phrase *redeeming the time* is also found in Colossians 4:5: "Walk in wisdom toward them that are without, redeeming the time" (KJV). In both passages, redeeming the time is related to wisdom in how we "walk," that is, in how we live.

Another way we can learn to redeem the time, is by asking God to help us. We should start every morning by committing our day to the Lord and asking Him to help us do something that day that has eternal significance. By beginning our day with eternity in mind, we become more aware of spiritual nudges in our hearts. We can look for ways we can honor God, help someone else, or utilize our time in productive ways. Traveling in our cars, sitting at a red light, we can pray for our neighbor. Cleaning our homes, mopping the floor, we can worship in song. At a restaurant, we can leave an extra big tip along with a gospel tract or a card inviting the server to church. We can evaluate our gifts and interests and find ways to invest them for God's kingdom.

Volunteering, serving at church, leading a ministry, taking Bible studies to the jails and prisons, and studying to show ourselves "approved unto God" are all ways we can redeem the time (2 Timothy 2:15, KJV). I'm applying the Pineapple Principle to my life.

Color in the Scriptures, Green and Yellow

When I think of pineapples, I think of a greenish-yellow fruit. The exterior of a pineapple changes from various shades of green to yellow as it ripens, so as a general rule, the more yellow a pineapple's exterior is, the riper the fruit will be.

While it is a mistake to ascribe some kind of spiritual or mystical message to every mention of a color in the Bible, there are definitely patterns of symbolism attached to some of the colors in the Bible. The different colors crop up again and again in Scripture, and we can learn certain things from the patterns we see.

During biblical days the color green was the emblem of freshness, vigor and prosperity. Psalms 52:8 (KJV)says "But I am like a green olive tree in the house of God: I trust in the mercy of God for ever and ever." Spiritually, green represents the color of life, abundance, renewal, growth and nature and energy. Green is a harmonizing, balancing and calming color. It's a healing color that gives healing energy to the heart.

In the book of Psalms 92:14 (NLT) the scripture says" Even in old age they will still produce fruit; they will remain vital and green". This scripture bears witness that even as we grow older, our value in the kingdom of God is not diminished. God has provided many examples of mature, older people in the scriptures who He used to perform great feats in their later years. 2 Corinthians 4:16 (KJV) say "For which cause we faint not; but though our outward man perish, yet the inward man is renewed day by day. As we age, our bodies get weaker, but the Holy Spirit renews our strength daily! Yes, vital and green!

Spiritually, the color yellow has stood for wisdom and intellect throughout the ages. The color supports our thoughts in logic, memory, concentration, will, as well as power and communication. Psalm 68:13 (KJV) "Though ye have lien among the pots, yet shall ye be as the wings of a dove covered with silver, and her feathers with yellow gold." The dove is a symbol of God's beloved Israel, who is so protected and blessed that it has taken silver and yellow gold from its enemies.

The Color Green in the Natural

The color green is a very down-to-earth color. It represents new beginnings and growth. It also signifies renewal and abundance. On the other hand, green can also represent envy or jealousy, as well as a lack of experience. Green has many calming attributes, but it also incorporates some of the energy of yellow. In design, green can have a balancing and harmonizing effect, and is very stable.

Green is also associated with growth, harmony, freshness, safety, fertility, and our environment. Traditionally, the color green is associated with money, finances, banking ambition, greed, jealousy and Wall Street.

The Color Yellow in the Natural

The color yellow represents warmth, cheerfulness, increased mental acuity, increased muscle energy. Yellow helps activate the memory, encourage communication, enhanced vision, build confidence, and stimulate the nervous system. Yes, I know that! I know this is true because I painted my kitchen yellow and the color makes me feel happy and enlightened every day! I'm reminded of the yellow in rainbows, Dorothy's yellow brick road and the words painted in yellow on the Black Lives Matter Plaza in Washington D.C! Yellow makes me feel immense happiness and joy!

Metamorphosis

The Greek word most frequently used for fruit καρπός (karpos). The word karpos is defined as the word fruit in the bible "the character of the fruit," being evidence of the character of the power producing it. Spiritual fruit is an expression of what is happening in a person's spirit or heart and how it manifests into actions, works, words, and attitudes, and how we love and serve others.

I believe God uses nature to teach us spiritual lessons to help us grow and mature. The metamorphosis of a caterpillar into a butterfly is one example and teaches us about our metamorphosis into mature Christian. Metamorphosis brings about a dramatic change in character or behavior of those who go through it. Metamorphosis is about evolution, rebirth, or transformation. It is about making corrections and realigning our lives to be what God has called us to be.

Unlike the caterpillar, this metamorphosis does not occur in the structure and the form of our DNA, but it takes place in our mind. Romans 12:2 (KJV) challenges us not to be a caterpillar all our lives, but to be transformed into a beautiful butterfly! God has called us to experience a spiritual metamorphosis!

Another example of metamorphosis in nature, is the metamorphosis process of a pineapple plant. The pineapple plant is grown from the top of the plant's crown (see How the Pineapple Is Grown in Section XIX). The plant roots, which are called suckers or shoots originate from stem which are at the base of the crown and will begin to grow and take root in about 2 months. Growing pineapples takes patience because it's a slow process; it takes about 18 months before the plant begins to mature. When the plant is ready to fruit, a stalk will appear in the middle of the leafy branches, which are called slips. The pineapple grows in the middle of the plant. This entire process takes about 3 years.

The term metamorphosis by definition means "a complete change of physical form or substance." In the animal world, it is "the marked and rapid transformation of a larva into an adult creature." It is miraculous to us that a worm-like creature crawling slowly across the ground could suddenly grow wings and fly gracefully in the summer sun. But God, in His infinite wisdom and power, designed that to happen over and over again in His created world. As I get older, I only wish God had designed a cocoon into which I could crawl and instantaneously restore some youthful energy and beauty. Unfortunately, that is not God's plan for us physically, but He has designed a metamorphosis of another kind for us.

However, unlike the butterfly, I believe that we experience various phases in the metamorphosis process continually throughout our Christian walk and not necessarily in any specific order. As human beings, we undergo an equally dramatic transformation, unfolding the path to liberation from within the depths of the soul and emerging, after great struggle, as an "expression of Jesus in the world".

In 2 Corinthians 5:17, (KJV) the Apostle Paul writes, "Therefore if any man be in Christ, he is a new creature: old things are passed away; behold, all things are become new." Spiritual metamorphosis is God's greatest desire and delight. He sent His Son into this world to die on a cross so that our old sinful nature could be changed into a new nature. All of us by nature are sinners and condemned to die, but God through His Son has provided a free gift of salvation whereby we might suddenly be made righteous in His sight.

"For if by one man's offence death reigned by one; much more they which receive abundance of grace and of the gift of righteousness shall reign in life by one, Jesus Christ," Romans 5:17, (KJV).

God wants to change us so that we are equipped to do His will and have the spiritual vigor to accomplish His work. This change cannot be manufactured or manipulated in our own power or through our own means. The caterpillar may desire to fly, but until it goes through the God-designed and God-created process of metamorphosis, it has no power to take to the skies. It is a miraculous change that cannot take place apart from the God our Father. Likewise, we may desire to go to Heaven when we die, but our only hope of doing so is by submitting to God's designed way of salvation. The Bible makes it very clear that spiritual metamorphosis only takes place one way.

Jesus said, "I am the way, the truth, and the life; no man cometh unto the Father, but by me" John 14:6 (KJV).

But while God's first goal for us is that immediate and instantaneous change that occurs at salvation, He also desires additional changes that occur through what the Bible calls sanctification (**see Section XII Steps to Sanctification**). These changes can take place rapidly or gradually, depending on our willingness to obey God's Word. Old habits and patterns of life that developed before salvation must now be replaced by new patterns fashioned by our conformity to God's image. This is why God has given us the body of Christ at our local church, and the people of God who minister to us the Word of God.

Ephesians 4:11 – 13 (KJV) says "And he gave some, apostles; and some, prophets; and some, evangelists; and some, pastors and teachers; For the perfecting of the saints, for the work of the ministry, for the edifying of the body of Christ: Till we all come in the unity of the faith, and of the knowledge of the Son of God, unto a perfect man, unto the measure of the stature of the fullness of Christ."

We naturally resist change. We don't like to give up the things that have fulfilled our flesh and satisfied our sinful appetites. The devil convinces us that to put off the old man and replace it with a new life in Christ is boring and unfulfilling. But quite frankly, it is just the opposite! Think of it this way: everyone likes a fresh change of clothes. Having to wear the same clothes every day would be boring and mundane. Most of us change our clothes often and even sometimes multiple times in a day. Those changes equip us for an upcoming activity or work, and often the simple changing of our clothes brings freshness to life and vitality to our purpose.

Sanctification involves the same process. We must daily allow God to strip us of those things' unbecoming to our Christian life and replace those old rags with robes of righteousness. Ephesians 4:22–24 (KJV) says, "That ye put off concerning the former conversation the old man, which is corrupt according to the deceitful lusts; And be renewed in the spirit of your mind; And that ye put on the new man, which after God is created in righteousness and true holiness."

So, take a look in the mirror. See yourself as God sees you. Allow yourself to be "metamorphosed" by the hands of God and live a new life with a new spiritual structure. Without Him, we're just a helpless worm groveling along on our path of sin. But God looks beyond who we are and has metamorphosis in mind! Crawl into His arms, and you will emerge a new creature in Christ.

After God has fed us His word, after we have rested in His presence, we experience a rebirth. We are empowered with our new perspective on life and will desire from deep within to make a difference in this world. We will fly and God will be the wind beneath our wings. Metamorphosis is a process which involves struggle, dissolving, reimagining, revising, and flying! It's not easy; however, when you emerge, spread your wings and fly!

By the way, when you're in the grocery store buy a fresh pineapple, cut it open and let its fruit inspire you that there's sweet victory on the other side of every conquered challenge!

Hallelujah!

CONCLUSION

Presented by Katherine T. Parker

The fruit of the Spirit is a clear reflection of God's love for us. The more we connect with the Spirit and the deeper our relationship with God grows, the easier it becomes to embody and reflect the fruit of the Spirit. As you move forward in assessing and applying the fruit of the Spirit to your life, I have summarized each fruit in three categories— *(1) Relationships towards God, (2) Social Relationships and (3) Christian Conduct that Guide Us.*

Relationship Towards God

While each fruit of the spirit symbolizes something different, the fruit of the Spirit I believe directly correlate with our relationship with God are *love, joy,* and *peace.*

The Greek word for **love** is "agape," meaning this is His nature, what He does and who He is. It is more than an emotion, but above natural affection and goodwill and benevolence to the just and unjust. This Christ kind of love will break down barriers to personal redemption and restoration to the saving of even your own soul. The commandment is that we love God with all our heart, soul, mind, and strength. This is the first and great commandment, then loving our neighbor as ourselves. There is no other commandment greater than these. The first and most important is our vertical love relationship towards God. Even at the 11th hour, there is still hope. This love lifestyle is a common thread that should influence willing obedience as your mode of operation to model Christ in the earth horizontally. As Christ hath loved us, we are to love one another, and it is the only sign to the world that we are His disciples. In keeping His commandments, we abide in His love. 1 Corinthians chapter 13 is a model for us to grow in the maturity of our love for Christ and each other, which is the greatest love of all. *Thank you, Lord, for your everlasting love. Please show us how to release your love without discrimination or disrespect, as you did for us. We dare not forget that you granted your love to us, while we were yet sinners and died for those that were lost. You were born of the Virgin Mary, crucified for our sins, rose from the grave on the third day, ascended, and now seated on the right hand of the Father. May we live a life that allows us to receive an invitation to come back to serve you. Being a constant example of God's love for us to take heed to a worldwide altar call, now you can come to Jesus!* It is a love that keeps on giving!

The Greek word for **joy** is "chara," which refers to a delight that we will experience in life, as we grow closer to Christ. It is a trust in joy that abides and remains in the most unfavorable circumstances that doesn't come from earthy things, but whose foundation is in God. As we obey, our joy will be full in Christ. As we receive the infilling of joy and peace in believing, we will abound in hope through the power of the Holy Spirit. It is by our faith that the unspeakable joy and full glory is ours!!! The joy of the Lord is our strength as we continue to trust it to be enough to receive it as our portion, at any time, as we carry our own cross!!!

The Greek word for **peace** is "arana," which means harmony, safety, prosperity, quietness, rest, exemption from rage, tranquility of heart is manifested. Jesus doesn't give peace as the world does, but it surpasses our understanding, and it keeps our heart and mind clear. Romans 5:1 (KJV) states, "Therefore being justified by faith, we have peace with God, through our Lord Jesus Christ." Romans 14:17 (KJV) says, "For the kingdom of God is not meat and drink; but righteousness, and peace, and joy in the Holy Ghost." Isaiah 26:3 (KJV), "Thou wilt keep him in perfect peace, whose mind is stayed on thee: because he trusteth in thee." We have peace in God, with God, through God, by our Lord and Savior Jesus Christ!! Let's follow peace with one another!!

Social Relationships

Social relationships refer to those connections to the people we interact with throughout our daily life. These relationships can include family, friends, coworkers, acquaintances and even strangers. No matter how you may define these relationships, it is important to carry the spirit of God with you for the duration of each one. It is only then, that we are guided spiritually and not by our flesh. The fruit of the spirit that I believe directly correlate to social relationships are *longsuffering, kindness,* and *goodness.*

The Greek word for **longsuffering** is "makrosthumia," which means enduring lasting hardships, long, distance, anger, swelling emotions, able to control one's thoughts or actions. Proverbs 16:32 (KJV) says, "He that is slow to anger is better than the mighty; and he that ruleth his spirit than he that taketh a city." Furthermore, Proverbs 25:28 (KJV) states, "He that hath no rule over his own spirit is like a city that is broken down and without walls,"— which leaves him open for attack!! As Christ has been slow to anger towards us, let us grant the same gift to one another. We are the city, so let's show God's glory in the earth!!! Help us Lord, as James states, "be swift to hear, slow to speak and slow to wrath."

The Greek word for **kindness** is "chrestotes," which means moral goodness, integrity, and gentleness. Psalms 18:35 (NKJV) says, "You have also given me the shield of your salvation; your right hand has held me up, your gentleness has made me great."

Because God is a loving Father and teacher, He makes heavy work an easy lesson. God corrects our mistakes with kindness. So, in glorifying God, let us be kind with others also!!!

The Greek word for **goodness** is "agathosyne," which means excellence of quality, uprightness of heart/life. Lord as mercy and goodness follows me all the days of my life, teach me how to follow you that I may show others your goodness also, the more excellent way that leads souls to you!!!

Christian Conduct Principles That Guide Us

The fruit of the Spirit can be considered guiding principles that we, as believers, should demonstrate regularly. It is these principles that can be a clear indication of not just our faithfulness, but an identifying factor as children of God. If we intentionally and purposefully apply the fruit of the Spirit to our lives and teach others to do so, they can clearly become spiritual principles that guide us. I would consider these principles to be *faith, gentleness*, and *self-control*.

The Greek word for **faith** is "pistis," which means I have a conviction that God exists and is the Creator and Ruler of all things, the Provider and Giver of eternal salvation through Christ in the Kingdom of God. I trust and have confidence in a true and living God that is trustworthy and consistent with His word and not a liar. So therefore, I live by faith, my faith with works, I still believe God against all odds and dismantle all other contrary voices. Come on faith, let's work things out, let's speak to some mountains, and let's frame our world. My faith is pleasing to the Lord, therefore, I have it right now for any situation. Keep your faith awakened and activated in God!!!

The Greek word for **gentleness** is "praoles," which means with love demonstrating mildness and humility. Galatians 6:1 (KJV) states, "Brethren, if a man be overtaken in a fault, ye which are spiritual, restore such an one in the spirit of meekness..." What is this, but the love of God?!!! The love that looks beyond one's faults and sees their needs! It is easy to harshly reprimand someone when you know that they have done wrong, it requires much more discipline and faith to admonish someone gently. If we are truly our brother and sister's keepers, who are we to judge, if we have not taught the right way to go? Gentleness is necessary for everyone; if we are to be Christ-like, it is important to always see the spirit of the person instead of the action.

The Greek word for **self-control** is "egkrateia," which means the power to master his own desires, passions, discipline to resist natural appetites, temptations and not conforming to the things of this world and allowing it to guide your decisions. Displaying self-control is a true way of honoring God and growing closer in your relationship with Him. When you focus on Him, you focus less on yourself, your wants, your desires and become more focused on your need and thirst for the Lord's presence in your life. Self-control helps to keep us grounded in our faith and truly focused on what is important—a life everlasting.

I trust the power of the Holy Ghost by way of effective prayer with faith, fasting, study, and meditation of God's Holy Word. I pray that the Lord instills in us a disciplined lifestyle, life of obedience, clothed in the armor of God with power and authority. It is with humility, submission, dedication, and commitment to His will that we will continue to hunger and thirst after His righteousness, that we might be filled with the fullness of the Godhead. We give you permission to drive out everything and deliver us from anything Lord God that will try to distract, destroy, or hinder, and abort our maturity in you. Lord God, deal with our worldly appetites and cravings, so we will thirst only for you. Please remove anyone and anything that will distract us from fellowshipping and communing with you!!! We esteem your Word above our necessary food, says Job. Jesus said in Matthew 4:4 (KJV), "Man shall not live by bread alone, but by every word that proceedeth out of the mouth of God."

Thank you, Jesus!!!

Now that you have taken this FRUIT OF THE SPIRIT journey with us, do you know ***WHAT FRUIT YOU ARE BEARING?***

You have embarked upon this journey with us, now I implore you to take what you know, take what you learned and be intentional. Be intentional, thoughtful, and purposeful in your actions, so that you can cultivate rich soil, sow good seed, and have a fruitful life. I admonish you to continue to be willing and obedient as you receive fresh instructions and new directions for the next steps in your life!!!

Be fruitful and multiply!!!

ABOUT THE AUTHORS

Carolyn W. Scott, Visionary

Pastor Carolyn W. Scott is a surrendered vessel and ambassador for the Kingdom of God. She has an Apostolic Kingdom anointing. She is not afraid to proclaim the works of her Lord and Savior Jesus Christ and will shout it whether in the valley low or on the mountain top! She has not always stood in this place of authority and confidence, but her journey has been proof positive, to the awesome works of Christ!

She worked for the Social Security Administration for 33 years, where she retired in 2003. She received salvation, March 5th, 1985 in a prayer group while at work at Social Security Administration. Her years at SSA were her training grounds. She was surrounded by a group of prayer warriors, who helped her to grow in Christ and encouraged her through her battle with cancer in 1985.

As she grew in her walk with Christ, she searched for a spiritual mother and father in the Gospel. All the while, God ended up making her a spiritual mother to many sons and daughters of the Kingdom.

Over the years she has been honored and blessed to be a part of several churches and outreach ministries as a servant leader, serving in several capacities, as needed. Today, she continues to play an intricate role in building the Kingdom of God as she has an undying commitment to put her hands to the plow.

Through her walk with Jesus Christ she is accustomed to being uncomfortable, feeling out of place and not fitting in. However, when in that place she realizes that she could not stay there and has learned how to press in, seek God, and war when necessary to get where the Lord really wants her to be!

She is often reminded of the day God spoke to her, saying "Think it not strange that I called you to be a pastor." She used to run away from her Kingdom calling and assignment, but today she stands to spread the good news of Jesus Christ as mandated in the Great Commission Matthew 28: 16-20. Today, God has given her a vision of the Fruit of the Spirit and has blessed her to oversee a fruitful bread outreach ministry serving the seniors.

She can be reached at **visionarycarolynwscott@gmail.com**.

Vonzella Faulk

Sister Vonzella Faulk originated in South Carolina; born into the union of the late Rev. & Mrs. Edward J. Brown. At the age of eleven, she was born again, baptized, and began to encompass a love relationship with The LORD and HIS Holy Word. She is the mother of two and a proud "Gammy" of six, plus one great-grandson.

Mrs. Faulk's love continues to bear fruit through her maternal compassion, as she mentors and coaches students in an early elementary school classroom. She remains actively involved in the choir, Praise Team, and Nurses Ministries at Cookley's Community Baptist Church, under the leadership of Dr. Mackie J. Cookley, Pastor.

Sister Vonzella Faulk also reveals her love for CHRIST through song writing, and has completed a CD project, entitled "Filled With Praise."

She can be reached at **ladefaulkv@gmail.com**.

Moniette S. Laury

Mrs. Moniette S. Laury is a Visionary, CEO, Evangelist, Senior Cosmetologist and takes no back seat in pursuing the dreams and plans the Lord has given her.

Over the years, she managed her own full-service beauty salon, formally known as Totally for You and Monet's Hair Gallery & Boutique. She has over 30 years of experience in the industry of beauty and fashion with a natural gift in beautifying the total woman.

Today, she continues to evolve and advance her business as Visionary & CEO of her very own cosmetic line, *Sara Sara Cosmetics*, custom jewelry line, *Mo L Designs* and costume jewelry and apparel line, *Sara Sara Beauty & Jewels*. You can regularly find her displaying her products and merchandise while sharing a word of inspiration and encouragement with her clientele.

Mrs. Laury is also founder of *My Cup Runneth Over (MCRO)Women's Outreach Ministry*, established in 2011 with a vision to cultivate and minister to young women as they evolve into the masterpieces God created them to be.

She is blessed to partner in business with her daughter, Mone't S. Horton as a dynamic mother-daughter team. Mrs. Laury gives all honor to God for the amazing support of her husband, Darrick Laury, mother Pastor Carolyn Scott, children, grandson, family and clients.

She can be reached at **moniettelaury@gmail.com**.

Carla B. Scott

Carla B. Scott is an anointed vessel and woman of God. She is a Certified Professional Makeup Artist who uses her creativity, gifts, and talents to positively impact the lives of those who come within her reach. She confidently stands in her calling with a passion to uplift and motivate young women.

She has had a love for the beauty industry since she grew up in her sister's salon. Over the years she fell in love with makeup artistry. Her passion grew stronger and she developed with every client who gave her an opportunity to put her skills to the test

In 2011, Ms. Scott relocated to Charlotte, NC from Baltimore, MD and was immensely blessed with the opportunity to work with models and designers for multiple fashion shows, photo shoots and plays. She then knew she could not give up on her gift and had to press forward to fulfill her passion. Her determination is evident through her desire to grow and continually increase her skillset.

Her work has been published in beauty, photography, and fashion magazines. In November 2014, she had the honor of being certified under the late Buntricia Bastian, International Beauty Industry Educator and her amazing team in Las Vegas, NV.

Ms. Scott's goal is to touch as many people as possible with her gifts and talents and she is determined to do just that!

She can be reached at **divahology@gmail.com**.

Mone't S. Horton

A spirit-led, purpose driven professional and inspirational coach, speaker, psalmist, author and entrepreneur Mone't S. Horton is a woman of many hats, gifts and talents. Her passion is to inspire individuals to fulfill their life purpose.

She is author of **From Reality to a Wealthy Place:** *The Fundamentals of Elevating Your Mindset to Live a Life of Abundance* (2017) and Co-Author of **Repositioned Crowns** (2017).

Miss Horton is the Visionary and Chief Inspiration Officer (CIO) of **Mo's Enterprise LLC** which houses *Connecting the Pieces (CTP) Coaching & Consulting Solutions, The Leading Ladies Empowerment Network, Sara Sara Cosmetics, Sara Sara Beauty & Jewels and Mo Fashions.*

Above all, Miss Horton serves as a mouthpiece, navigator, vessel, conduit, and resource to inspire and empower individuals, young and wise, man, woman, boy or girl to **powerfully**, and **unapologetically** connect the pieces of their lives to take ACTION and MANIFEST beyond what they can see. She believes that *all YOU need is Within YOU—NOW, is the time to Tap IN!* Through her own journey she has learned to embrace the process of life, stay in position, tap into her inner strength, remain Unstoppable and Manifest!

Miss Horton is given to and values Professional Excellence, Inspiration and Mentorship. She will empower you to *MOVE from your REALITY to your WEALTHY PLACE!*

She can be reached at **www.mos-enterprise.com**.

Jacqueline Ejim

Dr. Jacqueline Ejim has managed to fulfill scripture in being "steadfast, unmovable, and always abounding in the work of the Lord" throughout life. After accepting the Lord Jesus Christ as her personal Lord and Savior and receiving the precious gift of the Holy Ghost; this virtuous woman of God became known for extending the Agape Love of God to everyone that she come in contact with.

She believes that one should not only talk the Word of God but also live their life according to the Word of God. She believes in helping others especially hurting people. She has exemplified this through her teachings and illustrations as an Evangelist, Missionary, Usher, Choir member, Pastor's Nurse, Pastor's Armor Bearer and Intercessory /Prayer Warrior and Community Outreach Worker with Peace and Love Ministries.

Dr. Ejim received her Evangelistic Training at The Evangelical Cathedral in Dundalk, MD. She received her Masters of Chaplaincy/Christian Education at School of Bible Theology Seminary and University in San Jacinto, Ca./Canadian Bible College and University in Canada, a Masters of Education in Rehabilitation Counseling at Coppin State University, A Doctorate of Philosophy in Counseling at Family Bible Ministries Institute. She currently fellowships at Abundant Life Church Pentecostal Church in Rosedale, MD under the leadership of Pastor David Reevers.

She can be reached at **ejimj33@gmail.com**.

Euphrasynia Love Cookley

Evangelist Euphrasynia Love Cookley is the daughter of the late Santa E. Wallace and Larry Andrews, Sr. and is the oldest of four children. She is a servant of God, a wife a mother, and a Mary Kay Beauty Consultant. On June 6th, 1997, she married Reverend Kevin James Cookley. On January 20th, 2005 she gave birth to her daughter, Victorye Love Cookley. Euphrasynia loves her husband and daughter very much and is committed to being the best wife and mother she can be. On March 28th, 1999, she was licensed to preach the gospel of Jesus Christ by her father-in-law, Pastor Dr. Mackie J. Cookley. Over the years she has served on various ministries including prayer ministry, women's ministry, youth ministry, marriage ministry, pastor's partners, and dance ministry. Euphrasynia loves the Lord! She has been through many trials and knows God to be everything He promised to be, a present help, provider, healer, way maker, keeper, father and friend! She enjoys worshipping the Lord and her desire is please God, be all He's calling her to be and do all He's calling her to do.

She can be reached at **lovecookley@aol.com**.

Desirée Fernandez

Sister Desirée Fernandez is a dependent daughter of God, our Sovereign Creator. Privileged to be born into a family devoted to serving in the Kingdom of God. In her youth she was groomed by her parents, Deacon John and Missionary Vonzella Perkins, to serve in the house of the Lord through the ministry of helps, hospitality, and fellowship. By the confession of her faith, Desirée was baptized and filled with the Holy Spirit. This began a journey in the hand of the faithful and loving Father.

It was this personal, abiding relationship that continues to share the testimony of CHRIST JESUS; concerning His greatness, love, truth and soon to return. She is a co-laborer prayerfully seeking unification of God's remnant believers and redemption of His lost sheep.

Sister Fernandez has serviced the Kingdom as Pastoral Aides, Trustee, Intercessor and Outreach Ministry. Her gifts and kingdom principles have overflowed in her professional career as a cosmetologist, entrepreneur, and an educator. She is owner of "Seize the Moment Inspirational Gifts, Inc." providing publications and products to the Christian community.

She has been married for twenty-one years and counting. She is the parent of four children and one grandson.

She can be reached at **myinspiredmoment@outlook.com.**

Andrea Taylor

"Now unto him that is able to do exceeding abundantly above all that we ask or think, according to the power that worketh in us," -Ephesians 3:20 KJV

Life's experiences taught Evangelist Andrea Taylor to embrace change no matter how hard it is when it comes from God. Through these experiences she developed the ability (fruit of the spirit) to demonstrate God's patience and love for people in need of a second chance.

Evangelist Taylor believes every negative experience in life can be turned into a positive. That our life's experiences and situations are to be used to demonstrate God's ability to restore and reestablish others through Christ Jesus. Andrea's desire is to equip, develop, and empower spirit filled leaders, to minister to the weak and downtrodden, to help them recognize the power and unction of the Holy Spirit, and to understand that through Christ Jesus all things are possible!

She can be reached at **andreadenisetaylor57@gmail.com**.

Katherine T. Parker

Apostle Katherine T. Parker is a native of Snow Hill, NC. She is the dedicated wife of 21 years to Minister James E. Parker, mother of eight children and grandmother of eight grandchildren.

She accepted the Lord Jesus Christ as her personal Savior on September 17, 1978 and was called, chosen and anointed to preach the gospel 6 months later. Having obtained help from God, she has continued until this day!!! Today, she is Visionary & Pastor of On Time Church Ministries (OTCM) Inc. (est. November 2002).

Over the years, she has diligently spent time traveling near and far serving & supporting several leaders in ministries in various towns, cities, states and abroad. Her missionary journey has allowed her to serve in several capacities as Sunday school teacher, choir director, women's fellowship leader, van driver, preacher of the gospel, assistant pastor, and ordained elder. Her current assignment, at the ordered place and appointed time, is ordained Elder and Associate Pastor at Grace Restoration Life Christian Fellowship (GRL) where Chief Apostle Samuel A. Wright III is the founder and servant leader.

Her heartbeat of gospel is serving the homeless, helpless, hopeless and hunger—***sowing a seed to meet the need and giving a hand up and not a handout.*** She is the Pastor of the GRL's Team Outreach Ministries (T.O.M.) serving residents of the Waverly community. T.O.M. shows the love of Jesus by serving those in need in the community with a special assignment to the elderly and seniors providing a number of services that include, but are not limited to food, clothing, referral resources, furniture, appliances, emergency food and community activities. These services are on an emergency, weekly, monthly, and yearly basics, city and statewide. She is forever thankful for the T.O.M. volunteers, donors and sponsors who believe in her vision, prayerfully, monetarily, and with a seed to meet the need!!!

Apostle Parker received her Associates Degree (AA) from Dominion Leadership University in June 2010.

She is the host of OTCM Radio Broadcast, "A Fax from Heaven" aired from local radio stations WBGR, 1400 AM, and Heaven 600. Her motto is from Ecclesiastes 3:1-8 "Everything and everybody will fall in line in Gods own time." IS THERE NOT A CAUSE? YES, IT IS!!! Show, tell and share the GOSPEL (Good News) of Jesus Christ!!! She is deeply committed to a cause greater than herself!!

She can be reached at **afaxfromheaven1102@yahoo.com**.

Reflections & Notes

Made in the USA
Middletown, DE
12 January 2021